Get started in
Indonesian

Safitri Widagdo

Get started in Indonesian

Safitri Widagdo

First published in Great Britain in 2016 by Hodder and Stoughton. An Hachette UK company.

Copyright © Safitri Widagdo 2016

British Library Cataloguing in Publication Data: a catalogue record for this title is available from the British Library.

Library of Congress Catalog Card Number: on file.

Paperback ISBN: 9781444175028

6

Typeset by Cenveo® Publisher Services.

Printed and bound in Great Britain by Clays Ltd, Elcograf S.p.A.

John Murray Learning policy is to use papers that are natural, renewable and recyclable products and made from wood grown in sustainable forests. The logging and manufacturing processes are expected to conform to the environmental regulations of the country of origin.

Carmelite House
50 Victoria Embankment
London EC4Y 0DZ
www.hodder.co.uk

Also available in ebook

Contents

Acknowledgements

The author wishes to warmly thank all those who made this book possible, in particular Cecilia Bembibre and the team at Hodder & Stoughton, Sarah Jane Lewis of One ELT, Dr Ben Murtagh, the SOAS Department of South East Asian Studies, and for their support and company, Capability and Jim. This book is dedicated to her family.

About the author

Safitri Widagdo was born in Jakarta, Indonesia, and grew up with one foot in an Indonesian household and another in the expatriate community. She has taught Indonesian language courses and translation seminars to adult learners and university students at SOAS, University of London. She has a degree in South East Asian Studies from SOAS and a degree in English Literature from the University of Chicago.

How this book works

Welcome to *Get Started in Indonesian*, a course designed for absolute beginners! Indonesian is a fascinating language and accessible even to those who are not regular language learners. Since it has absorbed various concepts and words from other cultures and languages including English, it is a language that many learners find both tantalisingly foreign and comfortingly familiar. Indonesian is also practical because it has to be. In Indonesia, it facilitates social life in a nation where people speak hundreds of different languages and have just as many different ways of living. Its practical and sensible patterns balance the challenges posed to learners by the differences between the formal and informal styles of speaking and writing the language. This book will provide you with a basic knowledge of spoken and written Indonesian in both styles. The goal is for you to be able to get a good grounding in the language and feel at ease in various situations.

Each unit in *Get started in Indonesian* is structured in the following way:

What you will learn identifies what you will be able to do in Indonesian by the end of the unit.

 Culture point presents an interesting cultural aspect related to the unit theme, introduces some key words and phrases, and includes a challenging question for you.

 Vocabulary builder introduces key unit vocabulary grouped by theme and conversations, and is accompanied by audio.

Conversations are recorded dialogues you can listen to and practice, beginning with a narrative that helps you anticipate what you will hear, a focusing question, and follow-up activities. In this book, there are two conversations in each unit.

 Language discovery uses a set of questions to aid you in your discovery of key language points found in the conversations and provides a corresponding set of explanations to guide you in mastering the ideas or language patterns. Read the notes and look at the conversations to see how the language is used in practice and to aid quicker learning.

Practice offers a variety of exercises to give you a chance to 'pull it all together' and make active use of both spoken and written Indonesian.

 Pronunciation draws your attention to either particular sounds you encounter in the unit or differences in the pronunciation of the thematic vocabulary.

 Speaking helps you review your understanding of what you've learned so far and personalise what you've learned. When you're not asked to prepare what you want to say, try to do the speaking activities spontaneously.

 Listening activities showcase different but thematically similar contexts in which you'll hear spoken Indonesian to increase your exposure to and understanding of the language.

 Reading and writing provides practice in reading everyday texts that you might encounter. It also includes an opportunity to create your own written text in Indonesian.

Go further encourages you to deepen your language ability, including your speaking skills, by expanding on the thematic vocabulary and language points in each unit.

 Test yourself helps you assess what you have learned. Do the tests without looking at the rest of the unit.

Self check lets you see what you can do in Indonesian after mastering each unit. When you feel confident that you've got what you want to out of the lesson, move on to the next unit.

Give yourself time to study the units at your own pace, and remember to make frequent and repeated use of the audio.

To help you through the course, a system of icons indicates the actions you should take:

 Note the culture tip

 Figure something out for yourself

 Listen and repeat the pronunciation

 Listen to the audio

 Speak Indonesian out loud

 Practise your reading

Have a go at writing

 Check your Indonesian ability (no cheating!)

As you work your way through the course, you will become familiar with studying on your own, looking things up and checking your Indonesian language ability.

The book also includes resources you can consult at any time, whether before you begin the course, after a pause in your studies, or while you're working on the units:

Pronunciation guide gives an overview of Indonesian sounds in relation to how they are spelled.

Useful expressions provides a quick reference for everyday phrases and numbers.

Review units allow you to consolidate what you have learned in previous units. There are three reviews: after Unit 3, after Unit 6, and after Unit 10. Use your performance in each review to decide whether you are ready to move ahead or if you should return to specific points in the book and refresh or consolidate your knowledge.

Answer key helps you monitor your performance and check your progress. It includes answers and model answers to activities in both the main teaching units and the review units.

Indonesian–English glossary allows you to quickly access the vocabulary that is presented in the course.

English–Indonesian glossary allows you to quickly access in English the vocabulary that is presented in the course.

Throughout the book, there are tips about social and cultural influences that will help you put Indonesian into context so that you have a better understanding of how to use the language. Additionally, you can find a variety of online resources that are accessible to beginners. They range from Indonesian learning sites hosted by various schools and universities to accounts on social media that are updated with new vocabulary or grammar points. Browse around and combine the online resources with this course to enhance your learning. Soon you will be ready to speak Indonesian and gain access to all that Indonesia has to offer, whether your interest lies in its people, culture, natural beauty, or promising business opportunities.

Selamat belajar!

The Discovery method

There are lots of philosophies and approaches to language learning, some practical, some quite unconventional, and far too many to list here. Perhaps you know of a few, or even have some techniques of your own. In this book we have incorporated the Discovery method of learning, a sort of DIY approach to language learning. What this means is that you will be encouraged throughout the course to engage your mind and figure out the language for yourself, through identifying patterns, understanding grammar concepts, noticing words that are similar to English, and more. This method promotes language awareness, a critical skill in acquiring a new language. As a result of your own efforts, you will be able to better retain what you have learned, use it with confidence, and, even better, apply those same skills to continuing to learn the language (or, indeed, another one) on your own after you've finished this book.

Everyone can succeed in learning a language – the key is to know how to learn it. Learning is more than just reading or memorizing grammar and vocabulary. It's about being an active learner, learning in real contexts, and, most importantly, using what you've learned in different situations. Simply put, if you figure something out for yourself, you're more likely to understand it. And when you use what you've learned, you're more likely to remember it.

And because many of the essential but (let's admit it!) challenging details, such as grammar rules, are introduced through the Discovery method, you'll have more fun while learning. Soon, the language will start to make sense and you'll be relying on your own intuition to construct original sentences independently, not just listening and repeating.

Enjoy yourself!

Learn to learn

1 Make a habit out of learning

Study a little every day, between 20 and 30 minutes is ideal. **Give yourself short-term goals**, e.g. work out how long you'll spend on a particular unit and work within this time limit. This will help you to **create a study habit**. Try to **create an environment conducive to learning** which is calm and quiet and free from distractions. As you study, do not worry about your mistakes or the things you can't remember or understand. Languages settle gradually in the brain. **Just give yourself enough time** and you will succeed.

2 Maximise your exposure to the language

As well as using this course, you can listen to radio, watch television, read online articles and blogs, or watch music videos online and follow the on-screen lyrics. Do you have a personal passion or hobby? Does a news story interest you? Try to access information about them in Indonesian. It's entertaining and you'll become used to a range of writing and speaking styles. In time you'll also find your vocabulary and language recognition deepening.

3 Vocabulary

Group new words under **generic categories** such as *food or family;* **situations** in which they occur such as, *restaurant: waiter, plate, menu, bill;* and **functions** such as *greetings, parting, thanks, apologising.*

Write the words over and over again. Keep lists on your smartphone or tablet, but remember to switch the keyboard language so the auto-correct function supports your learning.

Listen to the audio several times and say the words out loud as you hear or read them.

Cover up the English side of the vocabulary list and see if you remember the meaning of the word. Do the same for the Indonesian.

Create flash cards, drawings and mind maps.

Write Indonesian words on post-it notes and stick them to objects in your environment.

Experiment with words. Look for patterns in words, for example, translate words based on how the word *reservation* appears in Indonesian as the word **reservasi**.

4 Grammar

Experiment with grammar rules. Reflect on how the rules of Indonesian compare with your own language or other languages.

Use known vocabulary to practise new grammar structures.

When you learn a new word, consider what other words you can turn it into. Could you turn a verb into a noun or an adjective into a verb if you apply what you know?

5 Pronunciation

Study individual sounds, then full words. Make a list of those words that give you trouble and practise them.

Repeat the conversations line by line and try to mimic what you hear. Record yourself if you can.

6 Listening and reading

The conversations in this book include questions to help guide you in your understanding. But you can do more:

Imagine the situation. Think about where a scene is taking place and make educated guesses – a conversation in a restaurant is likely to be about food.

Guess the meaning of key words before you look them up. When there are key words you don't understand, try to guess what they mean from the context.

7 Speaking

Practice makes perfect. The most successful language learners know how to overcome their inhibitions and keep going.

When you conduct a simple transaction with a salesperson, clerk or waiter, pretend that you have to do it in Indonesian, e.g. paying for your shopping, ordering food, getting directions and so on.

Rehearse the dialogues out loud, then try to replace sentences with ones that are true for you.

When asked to prepare answers to questions in speaking exercises, prepare more than one answer to each question to give yourself more material to practise with.

8 Learn from your errors

Making errors is part of any learning process, so don't be so worried about making mistakes that you won't say anything unless you are sure it is correct. This leads to a vicious circle: the less you say, the less practice you get and the more mistakes you make.

Note the seriousness of errors. Many errors are not serious as they do not affect the meaning.

9 Learn to cope with uncertainty

Take a chance. Don't let the need to choose between informal and formal ways of speaking stop you from practising. You will not be held up to the same standard of propriety as a native speaker would be. Also remember that in every social situation you can always take cues from how others are speaking and adjust your way of speaking accordingly.

Don't give up if you don't understand. If at some point you feel you don't understand what you are told, try to guess what is being said and keep following the conversation a while. Remember that in real life, the speaker might repeat or paraphrase what you didn't understand and the conversation can carry on.

Keep talking. The best way to improve your fluency in Indonesian is to seize every opportunity to speak. If you get stuck for a particular word, don't let the conversation stop; paraphrase or use the words you do know, even if you have to simplify what you want to say.

Don't over-use your dictionary. If you are also using a dictionary, resist the temptation to look up every word you don't know. Read the same passage several times, concentrating on trying to get the gist of it. If after the third time some words still prevent you from making sense of the passage, look them up in the dictionary.

Pronunciation guide

You'll be glad to know that with some exceptions, Indonesian pronunciation is very straightforward. The language also shares many sounds with English, even if some are spelled differently, and contains only one ambiguous sound **e**.

 00.01 Vowels

a	**lima**	*five*	the 'a' in car with the mouth open wider
i	**tiga**	*three*	the 'ee' in leech or the 'i' in chin
u	**buku**	*book*	the 'oo' in book
e	**empat**	*four*	a schwa or the 'e' in father
é	**pena**	*pen*	the 'e' in bet
o	**orang**	*person*	the 'o' in lot or the 'ou' in bought
aa	**maaf**	*sorry*	pronounced as two separate 'a' sounds
ai	**pantai**	*beach*	the vowel sound in bye
au	**danau**	*lake*	the vowel sound in wow
oi	**letoi**	*tired*	the vowel sound in toy

> Children in Indonesia learn the sequence of vowels as a, i, u, e, o. You can use this sequence to prompt you to think of vowels as they are pronounced in the Indonesian way.

The letter **e** can be pronounced as **e** or **é** in Indonesian. The old spelling showed the difference, but the current spelling does not distinguish between them. When you're not sure about how to pronounce a word you can say it as if you are asking a question and receive feedback from the person you're speaking to.

00.02 Consonants

Consonants pronounced as in English

b	**bayi**	*baby*
d	**dua**	*two*
g	**gang**	*alley*
h	**hari**	*day*
j	**jalan**	*street*
m	**mata**	*eye*
n	**nama**	*name*
ng	**ngeri**	*scary*
s	**salah**	*wrong*
w	**wajan**	*wok*
y	**ya**	*yes*

Consonants with a difference

c	**cepat**	*quick*	the 'ch' in chop
f	**feri**	*ferry*	like the English 'f' but sometimes as 'p'
k	**kota**	*city*	like the English 'k' but without aspiration
kh	**khas**	*typical*	the 'ch' in loch but sometimes as 'k'
l	**lagi**	*more*	the light English 'l' such as the 'l' in like
ny	**nyala**	*ablaze*	the 'ny' in onion
p	**pas**	*exact*	like the English 'p' but without aspiration
r	**roti**	*bread*	the rolling or rolled 'r'
sy	**syal**	*shawl*	pronounced as spelled or as 'sh'
t	**toko**	*shop*	like the English 't' but without aspiration
v	**vespa**	*scooter*	like the English 'f' but sometimes as 'p'

THE OLD SPELLING

Indonesian has undergone several spelling reforms, but the old spelling is still here today in place names, people's names, and iconic name brands. **Soekarno**, for example, is the old spelling of **Sukarno.**

the old spelling		the new spelling		
oe	**lampoe**	u	**lampu**	*light, lamp*
tj	**tjerita**	c	**cerita**	*story*
dj	**Djakarta**	j	**Jakarta**	*Jakarta*
é	**énak**	e	**enak**	*delicious*
j	**sjair**	y	**syair**	*quatrain*
nj	**njala**	ny	**nyala**	*ablaze*
sj	**sjukuran**	sy	**syukuran**	*thanksgiving*
ch	**achir**	kh	**akhir**	*end*

Now that a number of older Indonesian texts such as historical documents and martial arts stories have been digitised and can be found on the internet, you can browse through them to find words in which **e** is written and pronounced as **é**.

00.03 Stress

Where the stress falls depends on where you are in Indonesia because of the influence of local languages or dialects. In many cases, the stress falls on the penultimate (second to last) syllable of a word. In a word with only two syllables, that would be the first syllable of the word.

empat   perem**pa**tan

Useful expressions

Greetings, partings and courtesies

halo	*hello,* (telephone greeting)
dah	*goodbye*
sampai bertemu lagi	*see you, until we meet again*
sampai besok	*see you tomorrow*
sampai nanti	*see you later*
Apa kabar?	*How are you?*
Kabar baik.	*I'm well.*
Ada apa?	*What's the matter?*
Tidak ada apa-apa.	*Nothing's the matter.*
permisi	*excuse me, pardon me*
silakan	*please, go ahead*
maaf	*sorry*
tidak apa-apa	*it's nothing, no worries*
terima kasih	*thank you*
sama-sama	*likewise, you're welcome*

Making yourself understood

tolong ulang sekali lagi	*please repeat once again*
tolong ulang pelan-pelan	*please repeat slowly*
Apa arti ...?	*What is the meaning of ...?*
saya tidak tahu	*I don't know*
saya tidak mengerti	*I don't understand*

Needing assistance

tolong	*please, help*
saya beralergi ...	*I have an allergy to ...*
tolong ambilkan bonnya	*please bring me the cheque*
numpang tanya ...	*may I ask ...*
bisa bicara dengan ...	*may I speak with ...*

Some useful phrases

Selamat tidur!	*Sleep well!*
Selamat makan!	*Enjoy your meal!*
Semoga cepat sembuh!	*Get well soon!*
Selamat ulang tahun!	*Happy birthday!*

Counting

In Indonesian, the basic units for numbers are between zero and nine. Larger numbers come in groups similar to those in English, such as **belasan** (*teens*), **puluhan** (*tens*), and **ratusan** (*hundreds*).

0	nol *or* kosong	10	sepuluh
1	satu	11	sebelas
2	dua	12	dua belas
3	tiga	13	tiga belas
4	empat	14	empat belas
5	lima	15	lima belas
6	enam	16	enam belas
7	tujuh	17	tujuh belas
8	delapan	18	delapan belas
9	sembilan	19	sembilan belas

20	dua puluh	25	dua puluh lima
21	dua puluh satu	26	dua puluh enam
22	dua puluh dua	27	dua puluh tujuh
23	dua puluh tiga	28	dua puluh delapan
24	dua puluh empat	29	dua puluh sembilan

100	seratus	500	lima ratus
1000	seribu	5000	lima ribu
10,000	sepuluh ribu	50,000	lima puluh ribu
100,000	seratus ribu	500,000	lima ratus ribu

In Indonesia, being familiar with large numbers is very useful because prices of everyday goods run into the tens and hundreds of thousands. You'll be pleased to know that composing large numbers in Indonesian is done in a similar way to how it is done in English. Start with the largest group, for example the **ribuan** (*thousands*), and move to the second largest, for example the **ratusan** (*hundreds*), then to the tens, and so on.

123,450 = 123,000 + 400 + 50

seratus dua puluh tiga ribu empat ratus lima puluh

one hundred (and) twenty three thousand, four hundred (and) fifty

1 *Selamat pagi! Aku Linda.*
Good morning! I'm Linda.

In this unit you will learn how to:
▶ *use greetings that suit the time of day.*
▶ *introduce yourself and others.*
▶ *say where you're from, where you live, and where you work/study.*
▶ *use the appropriate pronouns when talking to others.*
▶ *thank others and respond to thanks.*

CEFR (A1): *Can introduce himself and others and can ask and answer questions about personal details.*

 ## Indonesian

Did you know that for many Indonesians, **bahasa Indonesia** (*Indonesian*) is not their first language either? An Indonesian usually belongs to an ethnic group whose language is his or her **bahasa ibu** (*mother tongue*). Indonesian is learned formally at school as the official language of the republic. It allows people of diverse cultural backgrounds across the archipelagic nation to communicate with one another. The roots of Indonesian lie in classical **bahasa Melayu** (*Malay*), but it is distinct from modern Malay due to the influence of **bahasa Jawa** (*Javanese)*. Periods of Dutch and Portuguese colonisation also left their mark, which is reflected in the use of informal expressions such as **halo** (*hello*) and **dah** (*goodbye*), and words such as **kantor** (*office*), **gereja** (*church*), and **keju** (*cheese*). Indonesian is a practical language in a region that has welcomed foreign traders and goods for many centuries and will continue to do so. It utilises borrowings from major world languages such as **bahasa Arab** (*Arabic*), **bahasa Cina** (*Chinese*), and **bahasa Inggris** (*English*). You will discover important differences between English and Indonesian, but you will also notice similarities that will help you.

 Look at the Indonesian words below. See if you can work out what they mean in English.

Eropa, Jepang, telepon, universitas, akuntan, dokter

Vocabulary builder

01.01 Look at the words and phrases and complete the English translations. Then listen to the recording and imitate the pronunciation of the speakers.

GREETINGS

Selamat pagi	*Good _____ (dawn to 10 a.m.)*
Selamat siang	*Good day (10 a.m. to 3 p.m.)*
Selamat sore	*Good _____ (3 p.m. to 6 p.m.)*
Selamat malam	*Good _____ (after sunset)*
	Goodnight
Permisi.	*Excuse me/us.*
Sampai bertemu lagi.	*Until (we) meet again.*

FORMAL PRONOUNS

saya	*I, me, my*
Anda	*you, your*

INFORMAL PRONOUNS

aku	*I, me, my*
kamu	*you, your*

> In Indonesian, pronouns such as *I, you*, and others become *my, your*, and others depending on where the pronouns are placed. In English, what tells you more about a noun such as *doctor* comes before the noun, for example, *my doctor*. In Indonesian, it is the reverse: what tells you more about the noun comes after it, so that when **saya** is used to mean (*my*), it comes after the noun, for example, **dokter saya** (*my doctor*).

ESSENTIAL WORDS

siapa	*who*	**apa**	*what*
mana	*where*	**dan**	*and*
ini	*this, these*	**itu**	*that, those*

LOCATION WORDS

dari	*from*
di	*at/in/on*
ke	*to*

NEW EXPRESSIONS

Kenalkan.	*Let me introduce (lit. acquaint) you.*
Silakan.	*Please./Go ahead.*
nama	*name*
Terima kasih.	*Thank you.*
Sama-sama.	*Likewise./You're welcome.*

Conversation 1

 01.02 *Mr Budi (Bapak Budi) runs into his colleague Mrs Wati (Ibu Wati) and Jonathan Curtis.*

1 Where does Jonathan live?

Wati	Selamat sore, Pak Budi.
Budi	Selamat sore, Bu Wati.
Wati	Kenalkan. Ini Jonathan Curtis.
Jon	Panggil saya Jon.
Budi	Saya Budi. Dari mana Anda berasal, Pak Jon?
Jon	Saya berasal dari Liverpool.
Budi	Anda tinggal di mana?
Jon	Saya tinggal di Jakarta.
Budi	Di mana Anda bekerja?
Jon	Saya bekerja di bank. Dan Anda?
Budi	Saya kerja di universitas.
Jon	Nama universitas Anda apa?
Budi	Universitas Palembang. Saya kolega Ibu Wati.
Wati	Permisi, Pak Budi.
Budi	Silakan.
Jon	Sampai bertemu lagi, Pak Budi!
Budi	Sampai bertemu lagi.

panggil	to call (by name)
berasal	come, originate
tinggal	live, reside
kerja	to work

When you're using **Bapak** and **Ibu** in everyday conversation to mean respectively (*Mr*) and (*Ms/Mrs*), they can be abbreviated to **Pak** and **Bu**.

2 Match the Indonesian to the English.

a Anda tinggal di mana?   1 *Until we meet again.*

b Permisi.   2 *Where do you come from?*

c Sampai bertemu lagi.   3 *Excuse me.*

d Dari mana Anda berasal?   4 *Where do you live?*

3 Read or listen again and answer the questions.
   a Around what time of day do you think it is?
   b Where is Pak Jon from?
   c Where does Pak Budi work?
   d What do you think **kolega** means?

4 01.03 **Now listen to the lines from the conversation and repeat. Be sure to pay attention to the pronunciation.**

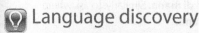 Language discovery

1 Find the sentences in the conversation that mean:
   a This is Jonathan Curtis. I am Budi.
   b Where do you work? I work at a university.
   c Where do you come from? Where do you live?

1 GETTING STARTED WITHOUT *IS, AM,* **AND** *ARE*

In everyday Indonesian, *I am Budi* or *this is Jon* is simply **saya Budi** or **ini Jon**. Similarly, **saya tinggal** is both *I live* and *I am living*.

2 WHAT YOU DO AND WHAT SOMEONE ELSE DOES

Unlike in English, verbs or action words, for example **bekerja** *work* and **berasal** *originate from*, do not change depending on who is acting.

Saya bekerja dan Pak Jon bekerja. *I work and Mr Jon works.*

When verbs appear in different forms, it's because of the use of affixes, word parts that are combined with root words to make other words. In Conversation 1, Budi uses both **bekerja** and **kerja** to mean *work*. **ber-** is a prefix, or an affix attached to the start of a word. When the root word is a verb, such as **kerja** *to work,* and there is no change in meaning, Indonesians will use either the root form or the proper form **bekerja** *work*. However, the root word of **berasal** is the noun **asal** meaning *origin* and this is only a verb when it is **berasal** *to originate from*.

> If the root word begins with **XerX** (where X is a consonant), such as **kerja** (*work*), the **ber-** prefix often loses its r, so that you end up with **bekerja** and not **berkerja**.

3 ASKING QUESTIONS

In Indonesian, there's no need to place question words, **mana** (*where*) and **apa** (*what*), at the start of the question.

Dari mana Anda berasal?	*From where do you come?*
Nama universitas Anda apa?	*Your university's name is what?*

However, **mana** (*where*) has to be used with the location word that matches the action. To ask where Jon came *from*, Budi used **dari mana**. To ask *in* what location Jon lives, Budi used **di mana.** Similarly, to ask where someone went *to*, you would use **ke mana.**

 ## Practice

1 **Put the following sentences into Indonesian.**
   a English is my mother tongue.
   b I am working in an office.
   c This is my colleague.
   d Utomo is living in China.

2 **Match the words to their root words.**

a	bekerja	1	temu
b	bertemu	2	bahasa
c	berasal	3	kerja
d	berbahasa	4	asal

 3 01.04 **Read the questions below and prepare responses that are true for you. Then, listen and respond in real time.**
   a Anda berasal dari mana?
   b Di mana Anda tinggal?
   c Anda bekerja di mana?
   d Apa nama bank Anda?

 ## Pronunciation

01.05 Let's begin with one of the most common sounds in Indonesian. Say aloud the English word 'back' and pay attention to the release of air at the end. When saying Indonesian words that end in the letter 'k', pronounce that 'k' without the release of air or aspiration. Listen to how the following words are pronounced and repeat.

1	bapak	3	masak
2	anak	4	bebek

 Speaking

Practise introducing yourself and others in Indonesian.

   a I'm …
   b Let me introduce you. This is …
   c My colleague is from …

Conversation 2

 01.07 Linda is sightseeing in Jakarta and sees an Indonesian girl whom she then approaches.

1 What is the name of the hotel?

Linda	Halo.
Girl	Halo.
Linda	Siapa nama kamu?
Girl	Nama aku Siti, Bu. Ibu siapa?
Linda	Aku Linda.
Girl	Ibu orang apa?
Linda	Aku orang Inggris. Siti, apa itu?
Girl	Itu hotel.
Linda	Apa nama hotel itu?
Girl	Hotel Indonesia.
Linda	Terima kasih.
Girl	Sama-sama.
Linda	Dah, Siti!
Girl	Dah, Bu Linda!

orang	*person*
Inggris	*England, English*

> When **Bu/Ibu** and **Pak/Bapak** are used on their own, they respectively mean *ma'am* and *sir*.

2 Find the expressions in the conversation that mean:
   a What is your name?
   b What is that?

c Thank you.

d You're welcome.

3 **Check, then cover up your answers and see if you can say them without looking at the conversation.**

4 **Read or listen again and answer the following questions.**

a What is the girl's name?

b Where is Linda from?

c Who is older or of higher status?

d Are they being formal or informal with each other?

5 01.08 **Now listen to the lines from the conversation and repeat. Then listen to Linda's lines and respond as Siti.**

Language discovery

1 **Refer to the conversation and choose the correct word:**

a *Apa / Siapa* nama kamu?

b Ibu orang *apa / siapa*?

1 WHO AND WHAT

You have now seen the question word **siapa** (*who*) used to ask for someone's name instead of the question word **apa** (*what*). This is a special case that applies only when asking for the names of humans, pets, or inanimate objects that have been given personal names by their owners. Note that when Linda asked for the name of the hotel, the word used was **apa** (*what*).

2 DESCRIBING YOURSELF

You can identify yourself and others as being a certain nationality, for example, English or American, by using the relevant place name with the word **orang** meaning *person*.

Kamu orang apa? Aku orang Inggris.

You are what kind of person? I am an English person.

Kamu orang apa? Aku orang Amerika.

What is your nationality? I am American.

Note that the question word **apa** (*what*) is placed after the noun **orang** (*person*), where the answer, in this case the place name, would be in your reply. In a question like this, the question word **apa** (*what*) needs to stay exactly where it is in relation to the word **orang** (*person*) or the question's meaning is lost. An alternative word order for this question is therefore,

Orang apa kamu?   literally, *What kind of person are you?*

 ## Practice

1 Give the Indonesian for the following questions.
   a What is your name?
   b What is the name of that university?

 2 01.09 Practise asking and answering questions about your nationality.

 Here are some countries where you may come from:

Skotlandia	*Scotland*	**Wales**	*Wales*
Irlandia	*Ireland*	**Kanada**	*Canada*
Singapura	*Singapore*	**India**	*India*
Australia	*Australia*	**Selandia Baru**	*New Zealand*

pamit	*take one's leave*	**pergi**	*go*
sekarang	*now*	**belajar**	*study*

 1 01.10 Listen to the following people as they greet or part from each other. Match each pair to the correct time of day.

a	Kris and Maria	**1**	11:00 p.m.
b	Wawan and Peter	**2**	06:00 a.m.
c	Heryanto and Wati	**3**	01:30 p.m.
d	Pingkan and Mimi	**4**	05:00 p.m.

> You can also use greetings that are related to the time of day as partings.

2 01.11 **Listen to the recording and complete the social media profiles.**

Name: _____   Hometown: _____
Location: _____   Education: _____

Name: _____   Hometown: _____
Location: _____   Education: _____

 3 01.12 **Read the questions below and prepare your own responses. Then, listen and respond in real time. Do this as many times as you need to for it to become second nature.**

Di mana kamu belajar?

Aku belajar di Universitas Indonesia.

a Siapa nama kamu?
b Di mana kamu tinggal sekarang?
c Dari mana kamu berasal?

Reading and writing

1 Read the blog entry and answer the questions.

> Halo. Nama saya Alex Lasut. Saya orang Indonesia. Saya berasal dari Sulawesi dan saya tinggal di Cardiff sekarang. Saya bekerja di Universitas Wales. Saya belajar di universitas itu.

a Alex orang apa?
b Dari mana Alex berasal?
c Di mana Alex tinggal sekarang?
d Di mana Alex bekerja dan belajar?

2 Write a blog entry about yourself.

Go further

When using Indonesian, you will need to think about whether you should be formal or informal, respectfully distant or close. Informal pronouns such as **aku** (*I*) and **kamu** (*you*) are used when speaking to friends, people of equal or lower status, and children. Using formal pronouns such as **saya** (*I*) and **Anda** (*you*), on the other hand, demonstrates respect to the person you're speaking to, perhaps because they are older or of higher social status. Pronouns are also chosen to fit the occasion, for example, when talking to people you've just met or in an office meeting. When in doubt, choose the formal pronouns.

Consider too that many Indonesians will be pleased to call you by your first name, but do not expect them to leave out the honorific **Bu** (*Ms/Mrs*) or **Pak** (*Mr*) unless they are older, of higher status, or a close friend. If you are an Emma or a Tom, for example, do get used to being **Bu Emma** or **Pak Tom**.

Indonesians might also describe themselves according to their regional or ethnic identity, whether due to their mother tongue, where their ancestors are from, or where they have spent most of their lives. Here are some of the larger ethnic classifications:

1 Match the Indonesian to the English.

a	orang Jawa	**1**	Madurese
b	orang Sunda	**2**	Batak
c	orang Melayu	**3**	Sundanese
d	orang Madura	**4**	Malay
e	orang Batak	**5**	Javanese

2 01.13 **Read the questions below and prepare appropriate responses. Then, listen and respond in real time. Do this as many times as you need to for it to become second nature.**

> Before the 1970s, the letter **u** was mainly spelled as **oe** in Indonesian. This spelling can still be found in Indonesian names.

a Pramoedya Ananta Toer orang apa?
b Siapa belajar bahasa Indonesia?

📝 Test yourself

1 Match the greeting to the times.
a	Selamat siang.	**1**	*08:00 a.m.*
b	Selamat sore.	**2**	*11:00 a.m.*
c	Selamat pagi.	**3**	*04:00 p.m.*

2 Give the English for the following sentences.
   a Kamu kerja di mana?
   b Saya bekerja di bank.
   c Bambang bekerja di Jepang.

3 Correct the underlined words.
   a Kamu belajar <u>dari</u> mana?
   b Pak Saud berasal <u>ke</u> mana?
   c Anda pergi <u>di</u> mana?

4 Complete the sentences.
   a _____ nama kamu?
   b _____ nama hotel Anda?
   c _____ orang itu?

5 Translate the following sentences into Indonesian.
   a I am Welsh.
   b My colleague is a New Zealander.
   c What is your nationality?

SELF CHECK

	I CAN . . .
⬤	. . . use greetings that suit the time of day
⬤	. . . introduce myself and others
⬤	. . . say where I am from, where I live, and where I work or study
⬤	. . . use the appropriate pronouns when talking to others
⬤	. . . thank others and respond to thanks

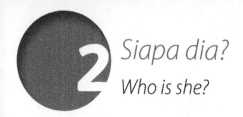

2 Siapa dia?

Who is she?

In this unit you will learn how to:
▶ *use the appropriate pronouns when talking about others.*
▶ *ask and answer yes/no questions.*
▶ *talk about events happening earlier or later in the day.*
▶ *ask for and give telephone numbers.*

CEFR (A1): *Can indicate time. Can introduce others. Can ask and answer questions about personal details.*

 ## Community

Many Indonesians enjoy socialising through a shared interest in an activity, whether it is cultural, recreational, or a sport. There are a variety of clubs at university for a student to join and where he or she can **bermain catur** (*play chess*), **menari** (*dance*), or **mendaki gunung** (*mountain climb*). It is in these clubs, and at their weekend trips and get-togethers, that a **kenalan** (*acquaintance*) can turn into a lifelong **teman** (*friend*). Outside the formal education system but equally important, there are local organisations where **orang-orang muda** (*young people*) can learn from their elders about **bermain musik tradisional** (*playing traditional music*) or **berlatih pencak silat** (*training in Indonesian martial arts*). A **kampung** (*village*), whether rural or urban, will have social events and cultural activities through which an Indonesian can mingle and get to know **tetangga dia** (*his/her neighbour*). Communities also hold **sepak bola** (*football*) and **bulu tangkis** (*badminton*) games, usually to celebrate Independence Day on the 17th of August, and all residents can participate as players or spectators. People who enjoy **berselam skuba** (*scuba diving*) and **berselancar** (*surfing*) may have to go to the coast or travel to the archipelago's smaller islands, but there enthusiasts can also gather and develop a sense of community that is very important in Indonesian life.

 How would you say *playing football* in Indonesian?

Vocabulary builder

02.01 **Look at the words and phrases and complete the English translations of contrasting adjectives. Then listen to the recording and imitate the pronunciation of the speakers.**

ADJECTIVES

ramah	*friendly, warm*	**sombong**	*snobbish*
lama	*old, of long duration*	**baru**	*new*
tua	_____	**muda**	*young*
tinggi	*tall*	**pendek**	_____

NEUTRAL PRONOUNS

dia	*he/she, him/her, his/her*
kami	*we/us/our (exclusive)*
kita	*we/us/our (inclusive)*

NUMBERS

0	nol *or* kosong		5	lima
1	satu		6	enam
2	dua		7	tujuh
3	tiga		8	delapan
4	empat		9	sembilan

NEW EXPRESSIONS

Apakah	*(interrogative in yes/no questions)*
ya	*yes*
juga	*too, also*
bukan	*no, not*
pulau	*island*
tidak	*no, not*
senang	*enjoy*
Ayo!	*Come! / Come on!*
kepada	*to (someone)*
harus	*must*
tadi	*earlier*
nanti	*later*
berapa	*how many*
nomor telpon	*telephone number*

Conversation 1

02.02 *Wati has brought Linda, who is talking to others, to a street party. Affandi is Wati's neighbour.*

1 What did Linda and Wati do on the island of Bangka?

Affandi	Selamat malam, Wati.
Wati	Selamat malam. Apakah Anda Affandi?
Affandi	Ya. Saya Affandi.
Wati	Kita bertetangga?
Affandi	Ya. Say a tetangga baru Anda. Wati, saya tidak kenal orang itu. Apakah dia tetangga kita juga?
Wati	Bukan. Dia bukan tetangga kita.
Affandi	Siapa dia?
Wati	Dia Linda, teman lama saya. Kami berkenalan di Bangka. Kami berselam skuba di pulau itu.
Affandi	Linda ramah?
Wati	Ya, Linda ramah. Dia tidak sombong.
Affandi	Dia senang apa?
Wati	Dia senang mendaki gunung dan berselam skuba. Dan Affandi?
Affandi	Saya senang mendaki gunung juga.
Wati	Ayo! Saya kenalkan Affandi kepada Linda.

bertetangga	*to be/become neighbours*
kenal	*recognise, know*
senang	*enjoy, be pleased*

2 Find the expressions in the conversation that mean:
   a I am your new neighbour. _____
   b Who is she? _____
   c What does she enjoy? _____
   d Come on! _____

3 Check, then cover up your answers and see if you can say them without looking at the conversation.

16

4 Read the conversation or listen again and answer the questions.

  a Around what time of day is it?
  b Is Linda their neighbour too?
  c Who enjoys mountain climbing?
  d What is Wati going to do?

5 02.03 **Now listen to the lines from the conversation and repeat. Be sure to pay attention to the pronunciation.**

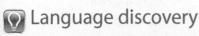 Language discovery

1 Look at the sentences from the conversation. Put the words in English into Indonesian.

  a Dia Linda, (*my old friend*).
  b (*We*) bertetangga. (*We*) berselam skuba di pulau itu.
  c Dia (*not*) tetangga kita. Dia (*not*) sombong.

1 WORD ORDER

In Indonesian, an adjective will come after the word it describes so that a *new friend* is a **teman baru.** When arranging the word order in a longer noun phrase such as *my old friend*, the order in Indonesian will be the reverse of the order in English so that you would say **teman lama saya**.

2 *WE*

Unlike other pronouns, **kita** or **kami** is used to mean *we, us, our* depending on whom you include or exclude from the grouping. You can use **kita** (*we, us*) when the person you're speaking to is included and **kami** when they are not. Linda used **kita** when she asked Affandi, **Kita bertetangga?** (*Are we neighbours?*) because he was included in the *we*. Linda used **kami** to mean Wati and herself, whilst telling Affandi, **'Kami berkenalan di Bangka'** (*We became acquainted in Bangka*) because he was not included in the *we*.

3 ASKING AND ANSWERING YES/NO QUESTIONS

You can turn statements into yes/no questions using **apakah** (*whether, if*) as the question word **Apakah**. If you are familiar with how a question sounds, you can leave out **Apakah**.

Kamu Affandi.	*You are Affandi.*
Apakah kamu Affandi? Kamu Affandi?	*Are you Affandi?*

To express *yes* in Indonesian, you can use the word **ya**.

Ya, saya Affandi.   *Yes, I am Affandi.*

There are two different Indonesian words for *no/not*. The word **tidak** is used to negate verbs and adjectives. The word **bukan** is used to negate nouns, including names and pronouns. They are both placed before what you are negating in the sentence.

Tidak. Aku tidak berselancar.   *No. I do not surf.*

Tidak. Dia tidak tinggi.   *No. He is not tall.*

Bukan. Dia bukan Affandi.   *No. He is not Affandi.*

Practice

1 Put the following sentences into English.
   a kenalan baru saya
   b teman pendek kami

2 Choose the correct word.
   a *Kita / Kami* bermain catur. (*said to Shinta, including Shinta*)
   b *Kita / Kami* menari. (*said to Shinta, not including Shinta*)

 3 02.04 Turn the statements below into yes/no questions using *apakah* **and prepare your own responses. Then, listen and respond in real time.**
   a Anda berlatih pencak silat di Indonesia.
   b Anda orang Indonesia.
   c Anda tinggi.

Pronunciation

 02.05 The consonant *ng* **is found in English at the end and middle of words, such as in 'singing' and 'mingle', but in Indonesian it is also found at the start of words. Listen to how the following words are pronounced and repeat.**

1 singa   **4** ngantuk

2 tetangga   **5** nganga

3 mangga

> If you're having trouble with words that begin with ng, try for example, to say the meaningless singantuk and then practise omitting the si at the beginning.

Speaking

 02.06 **Practise telling others about one of your friends and tell them about what you and your friend enjoy doing together. Use what you know instead of looking up new words. Here are some other activities to help you.**

berenang	*swimming*
membaca	*reading*
minum-minum	*drinking (alcoholic beverages)*
makan-makan	*eating (for pleasure)*

> Dia ... Dia orang ... Kami senang ...

Conversation 2

 02.07 *Budi and Jon meet again but Jon is in a rush. Budi would like Jon's phone number.*

1 What is Jon's telephone number?

Budi	Anda harus berbuat apa sekarang?
Jon	Saya harus bekerja sekarang. Saya berselancar tadi pagi. Nanti malam kita bertemu lagi?
Budi	Saya berlatih pencak silat nanti malam. Anda senang pencak silat?
Jon	Ya. Saya senang pencak silat.
Budi	Berapa nomor telpon Anda?
Jon	Nomor telpon saya kosong – delapan – satu – satu – tujuh – empat – enam – dua – lima – tiga – dua – sembilan.
Budi	Ini nomor ponsel Pak Jon?
Jon	Ya. Itu nomor ponsel saya.
Budi	Saya menelpon Pak Jon nanti sore.
Jon	Sampai nanti sore.

berbuat	*do (something)*
ponsel	*cell phone*
menelpon	*call* (v.), *ring* (v.)

> Indonesians are fond of acronyms, so much so that there are whole dictionaries devoted to them. One popular acronym for the *cell phone* **ponsel** is taken from the last syllable of **telpon** and the first syllable of **seluler**. Equally widespread is **HP**, short for *hand phone*.

2 Match the Indonesian to the English.

a	tadi pagi	**1**	*later tonight*
b	sekarang	**2**	*later this afternoon*
c	nanti sore	**3**	*earlier this morning*
d	nanti malam	**4**	*now*

3 Read or listen again and answer the following questions.

a When did Jon go surfing?
b When is Budi practising martial arts?
c When will Budi call Jon?
d What time of day do you think it is?

4 02.08 **Now listen to the lines from the conversation and repeat. Then listen to Budi's lines and respond as Jon.**

 Language discovery

1 Look at the sentences from the conversation. Find the words in Indonesian for the words in English.

a Saya berselancar (*earlier this morning*).

b (*What*) nomor telpon Anda? Saya menelpon (*you*) nanti sore.

1 LATER AND EARLIER

You can use the words **nanti** (*later*) and **tadi** (*earlier*) on their own, but Indonesians also combine them with the times of day to talk about different time periods in that day.

tadi pagi	*earlier in the morning* (dawn to 10 a.m.)
tadi siang	*earlier during the day* (10 a.m. to 3 p.m.)
tadi sore	*earlier in the afternoon* (3 p.m. to 6 p.m.)
nanti siang	*later during the day* (10 a.m. to 3 p.m.)
nanti sore	*later in the afternoon* (3 p.m. to 6 p.m.)
nanti malam	*later in the evening, later tonight* (after sunset)

Note that since all of these times occur in the same 24-hour period as the current time of day, you cannot say **nanti pagi** (*later in the morning*) but you can say **tadi malam** to mean *last night*.

2 ASKING FOR A TELEPHONE NUMBER

The question word **berapa** (*how many*) is used whenever the answer is a number, even when there is no counting involved. When asking for a telephone number, you would use **berapa** instead of **apa** (*what*).

3 USING SOMEONE'S NAME TO MEAN YOU

Often, **Anda** and **kamu** (*you*) can be replaced with the name of the person being spoken to. For example, Budi switched from using **Anda** to **Pak Jon** to mean *you* towards the end of Conversation 2. Budi asked **'Ini nomor ponsel Pak Jon?'** *This is Mr Jon's cell phone number?* to actually mean *This is your cell phone number?*. It is a way of speaking that is useful when social status is unclear or when formal pronouns prohibit a sense of closeness and friendliness.

 Practice

1 Put the following sentences into Indonesian.
  a I was playing traditional music this morning and last night.
  b He is playing badminton later this afternoon.

 2 02.09 **First, practise asking and answering questions about your phone number. Then, replace** *Anda* **or** *kamu* **in the question with your name and practise again.**

 Listening

rumah	house, home	teras	porch
halaman	yard, garden	sekolah	school

1 02.10 **Listen to the dialogue and answer the following questions.**
  a Where did they play football?
  b Where are they playing chess?
  c When will they go out to eat?

2 02.11 **Listen to the recording and write down Ratna's telephone numbers.**

> Ratna HP: _____
> Kantor: _____
> Rumah: _____

3 02.12 **Read the questions below and prepare your own responses. Then, listen and respond in real time. Do this as many times as you need to for it to become second nature.**

  a Apakah teman kamu muda?

  b Kamu harus berbuat apa sekarang?

  c Berapa nomor telpon kamu?

 Reading and writing

1 Linda is currently living in Indonesia. She has written a blog post about her time in Indonesia so far. To practise her language skills, she has chosen to write it in Indonesian. Read the post and check the glossary if there are words you don't know.

Halo dari Indonesia!

Wati teman lama saya. Saya berkenalan dengan Wati di Pulau Bangka di mana kami berselam skuba. Wati orang Jawa. Dia dari Yogyakarta. Dia tinggi, gemuk, dan ramah. Kami senang menari dan bermain musik tradisional. Tadi malam saya pergi ke rumah dia di kampung Kauman. Kami menari dan makan-makan di rumah tetangga dia. Saya berkenalan dengan Affandi. Dia teman baru saya. Nanti sore kami bermain bulu tangkis.

Sampai nanti!

2 Imagine you are writing a blog post about your time in Indonesia. Describe your Indonesian friends and how you met them.

Go further

Like the neutral pronoun **dia**, the very formal **beliau** is used to talk about both male (*he/him/his*) and female (*she/her*) others. However, it's most often used in the news or when referring to someone of much higher status, such as a venerable elder. In everyday formal situations, using the person's name instead of pronouns when referring to him/her is more common.

Beliau kepala negara di negara ini.

He/she is the head of state in this country.

In this Unit, you've seen verbs that begin with the prefix **meX-,** such as **menelpon** (*ring*) and **mendaki** (*climb*). The **X** in **meX-** stands for a consonant that changes depending on the root word. (If you'd like to read ahead about how the consonants change, you can go to Unit 8.) The prefix **meX-** is generally used when the verb describes an action that involves more than just the actor. For example, you ring *someone* and you climb *something*.

You now know that the word **senang** can mean *to enjoy* and *to be pleased*. If an activity *pleases* you because it is fun or pleasurable, you can say it is **menyenangkan** *pleasing*.

1 Use the words in the box to recreate the sentences below.

> senang, bermain, ke, senang, saya, Indonesia,
> saya, menyenangkan, pergi, gamelan

- **a** I am pleased.
- **b** Playing gamelan is fun.
- **c** I enjoy going to Indonesia.

There are many different instruments in Indonesian traditional music. One of the most impressive is the **gamelan**, which is actually an ensemble of drums and bronze percussions. Another is the Sundanese **angklung**, a set of bamboo tubes arranged on a frame and shaken to produce repeating notes.

---

2 02.13 **Read the questions below and prepare your own responses. Then, listen and respond. Do this as many times as you need to for it to become second nature.**
- **a** Apakah musik tradisional negara Anda menyenangkan?
- **b** Apakah bertemu orang Indonesia menyenangkan?

? Test yourself

1 Put the following sentences into Indonesian.
  a He is my new neighbour.
  b This is her school's phone number.
  c That is my house's porch.

2 Imagine you are speaking to Jon. Use the correct form of *we* to replace the words in English.
  a *(You and I)* berlatih pencak silat nanti malam.
  b *(Wati and I)* berasal dari Indonesia.
  c *(You and I)* berteman.

3 Put the words in English into Indonesian.
  a *(No.)* Saya *(not)* bermain catur.
  b Teman dia *(not)* tua.
  c *(No)*. Dia *(not)* tetangga saya.

4 Match the Indonesian to the English.
  a tadi sore   **1** *later this evening*
  b nanti sore   **2** *earlier this afternoon*
  c tadi malam   **3** *later this afternoon*
  d nanti malam   **4** *last night*

5 Complete the English translations.
  a nomor telpon   *telephone* _____
  b ponsel   _____
  c Berapa nomor HP Anda?   _____

6 Imagine you are asking Linda the following questions. Where possible, replace the pronouns with her name.
  a Ke mana aku dan kamu pergi sekarang?
  b Di mana dia bertemu kamu?
  c Anda dan dia berselam skuba di mana?

SELF CHECK

	I CAN ...
○	use the appropriate pronouns when talking about others
○	ask and answer yes/no questions
○	talk about events happening earlier or later in the day
○	ask for and give telephone numbers

3

Apa kabar keluarga Anda?
How is your family?

In this unit you will learn how to:
- *ask and answer questions about how you and others are.*
- *talk about your family.*
- *indicate whether you have or have not done something.*
- *make a phone call, and leave and take a message.*
- *indicate if you are (not) following the conversation.*

CEFR (A1): *Can recognize familiar words concerning self and family. Can ask how people are and react to news.*

 Family

Contemporary Indonesian society, with the **keluarga** (*family*) at its heart, remains shaped by traditional values and gender roles. It is assumed that everyone will marry one day and have **anak-anak** (*children*). When Indonesians ask whether someone is **belum menikah** (*not yet married*) or **sudah menikah** (*already married*) not long after meeting him or her for the first time, they would not think of themselves as nosy or forward. This is perhaps easier for someone to **mengerti** (*understand*) when he knows that questions about his marital status are meant to reflect an interest in his life's fulfilment. It is thought that to become a **bapak** or **ayah** (*father*) and **ibu** (*mother*) is to realise one's potential as a **laki-laki** (*man, male*) and a **perempuan** (*woman, female*). Public health programs advocate having only **dua anak** (*two children*), but having more children is common because a large family is thought to be a blessing. This includes having several generations living together, with offspring continuing to share a household with their **orang tua** (*parents*) even after marriage or staying nearby so that both the **kakek** (*grandfather*) and **nenek** (*grandmother*) have a role in the upbringing of children.

 If **anak-anak** is the word for children, what do you think the word for families might be in Indonesian?

Vocabulary builder

03.01 Look at the words and phrases and complete the English translations. Then listen to the recording and imitate the pronunciation of the speakers.

FAMILY MEMBERS

suami	*husband*
istri	*wife*
adik	*younger sibling*
adik-adik	_____
kakak	*older sibling*
kakak-kakak	_____
cucu	*grandchild*
cucu-cucu	_____

> The all-encompassing word **saudara** (*relative/sibling*) also signals close ties between people who are only distantly related or who are not related by blood.

TEMPORAL MARKERS

sudah	*already*
belum	*not yet*
masih	*still*

TIME

hari ini	*today* (lit. *this day*)
kemarin	*yesterday*
besok	*tomorrow*

PLURAL PRONOUN

mereka	*they, them, their*

NEW EXPRESSIONS

Apa kabar?	*How are you?* (lit. *What news?*)
Kabar baik.	*I'm well.* (lit. *Good news.*)
Kasihan!	*What a pity!, Poor thing!*
punya	*have, possess, own*
Oh begitu.	*Oh I see.* (lit. *Oh it's like that.*)
bisa	*can, able to*
bicara	*speak, converse*
dengan	*with*
titip pesan	*entrust a message*
Tolong ulang	*Please repeat*
sekali lagi	*one more time* (lit. *once more*)
Baiklah.	*All right., Okay.*

Conversation 1

03.02 *Budi and Jon meet again and find out more about each other.*

1 Who is not yet married?

Jon	Selamat siang, Pak Budi.
Budi	Selamat siang, Pak Jon.
Jon	Apa kabar?
Budi	Kabar baik, Pak Jon. Dan Anda?
Jon	Saya baik juga. Apa kabar keluarga Anda?
Budi	Anak saya baik. Istri saya tidak baik kemarin.
Jon	Kasihan! Beliau masih sakit hari ini?
Budi	Tidak. Dia sudah sembuh. Dia baik pagi ini.
Jon	Bagus!
Budi	Pak Jon sudah menikah?
Jon	Belum. Saya belum menikah.
Budi	Oh begitu. Orang tua Pak Jon di Inggris sudah punya cucu?
Jon	Sudah. Mereka sudah punya cucu-cucu. Kakak laki-laki saya sudah punya tiga anak perempuan.
Budi	Bagus! Di mana mereka tinggal?
Jon	Keluarga kakak saya tinggal di Irlandia.

baik	*good, well*
bagus	*good, well done*
sakit	*ill, sick*
sembuh	*recover, get well again*

2 Find the expressions in the conversation that mean:
   a Poor thing!   _____
   b How are you?   _____
   c Good!   _____
   d How is your family?   _____

3 Check, then cover up your answers and see if you can say them without looking at the conversation.

4 Read the conversation or listen again and answer the questions.
   a Around what time of day is it?
   b Who was unwell?
   c How many grandchildren do Jon's parents have?
   d Who lives in Ireland?

5 03.03 **Now listen to the lines from the conversation and repeat. Be sure to pay attention to the pronunciation.**

 Language discovery

1 Look at the sentences from the conversation. Put the words in English into Indonesian.
  a Kabar (*good*).
  b Saya (*well*) juga.
  c (*Good*)!

2 Refer to the conversation. Put the following sentences into Indonesian.
  a I am not yet married.
  b They already have grandchildren.

1 ASKING AND RESPONDING TO HOW OTHERS ARE

When you ask someone how they are, you're asking for their **kabar** (*news*). If someone is *well* or their news is *good*, they will use the word **baik**, which is generally used to talk about wellness, niceness, and things humans can't control, such as one's news. To give a positive response to someone's news, you can use the word **bagus** (*good*), which is used when praising human achievements, products, or favourable developments, such as being well or recovering from an illness. When you want to express sympathy about others, you can say **Kasihan!** (*Poor thing!*). When you want to give a neutral reply, you can say **Oh begitu** (*Oh it's like that*) to mean *Oh I see*.

2 WHAT HAS OR HAS NOT HAPPENED

Whether something has happened, is still happening, or has not yet happened, the Indonesian verb stays the same. In order to be able to express these different states, you should use temporal markers before the verb, such as **sudah** (*already*), **masih** (*still*), and **belum** (*not yet*).

As in English, the words **sudah** (*already*) and **belum** (*not yet*) negate each other. When you want to use **tidak** (*not*) with a marker, you place it before the marker.

Saya belum bekerja.	*I have not worked yet.*
Saya masih bekerja.	*I am still working.*
Saya sudah bekerja.	*I already worked.*
Saya tidak masih bekerja.	*I am not still working.*

At social gatherings, Indonesians may greet you by asking **Sudah makan?** meaning (*Have you eaten?*).

Practice

1 Put the following sentences into English.
- **a** Apa kabar?
- **b** Saya baik.

2 03.04 **Read the questions below and prepare your own responses. Then, listen and respond in real time.**
- **a** Anda sudah menikah?
- **b** Anda belum punya cucu?

Pronunciation

03.05 **When AI and AU are found in syllables that end in a vowel, they form combinations so that AI sounds like the vowel in 'pie' and AU sounds like the vowel in 'how'. When AI and AU are found in syllables that end in a consonant, however, they don't form a combination and are pronounced separately instead. Listen to how the following words are pronounced and repeat.**

1 sampai   **2** bagaimana   **3** baik

4 saudara   **5** beliau   **6** laut

Speaking

1 03.06 **Look at the family tree and describe each relationship in a sentence.**

Edwin dan Mutia orang tua Hendri.

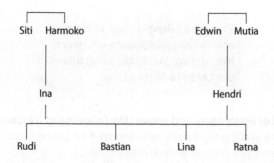

2 Dan keluarga Anda? *And what about your family?* **Describe the same relationships between people in your family.**

 Conversation 2

03.07 *Budi is calling Jon, but Saul answers instead.*

1 Who is Saul?

Budi	Halo. Bisa bicara dengan Pak Jon?
Saul	Halo. Tidak bisa. Jon masih bekerja. Dengan siapa saya berbicara?
Budi	Ini Budi.
Saul	Oh, Pak Budi! Anda teman kakak saya.
Budi	Oh saya tidak tahu Pak Jon punya adik di Indonesia.
Saul	Ya. Jon punya dua adik. Saya tinggal di Indonesia juga dan Thomas tinggal di Inggris.
Budi	Oh begitu. Saya bisa menitip pesan?
Saul	Saya tidak mengerti. Tolong ulang sekali lagi.
Budi	Bisa titip pesan? *Can I leave a message?*
Saul	Saya mengerti sekarang. Bisa. Apa pesan Anda?
Budi	Tolong bilang, 'Budi menelpon Pak Jon besok.'
Saul	Baiklah. Nanti saya sampaikan.
Budi	Terima kasih.
Saul	Sama-sama.

tahu	know, be aware (of)
Halo	(telephone greeting)
bilang	say
sampaikan	pass (something) on

> The word **bilang** is used to mean *say* only in colloquial speech or speech-like writing. You would otherwise use **berkata** to mean *say*.

2 Read or listen again and answer the following questions.
   a Why was Jon not the one who answered the phone?
   b How many younger siblings does Jon have?
   c What did Saul ask Budi to do when he didn't understand him?
   d What is Budi's message?

3 Match the Indonesian to the English.
   a Bisa bicara dengan Pak Jon?   1 *All right.*
   b Saya tidak mengerti.   2 *Can I leave a message?*
   c Bisa titip pesan?   3 *I don't understand.*
   d Baiklah.   4 *Can I speak to Mr Jon?*

4 03.08 **Now listen to the lines from the conversation and repeat. Then listen to Budi's lines and respond as Saul.**

Language discovery

1 Refer to the conversation and put the following sentences into Indonesian.
   a I will call him tomorrow.
   b two younger siblings
   c Please say, 'I understand now'.

1 THE IMPORTANCE OF TIME WORDS

As you may have noticed, Indonesian verbs do not change in response to time. There are no tenses to worry about, but you do then have to rely on words like **kemarin** (*yesterday*), **hari ini** (*today*), and **besok** (*tomorrow*) to make your meaning clear.

2 PLURALS AND NUMBERS

To create the plural form, you simply repeat the noun, adding a hyphen between them in written Indonesian. For example, **cucu** is *grandchild* and **cucu-cucu** is *grandchildren*. This is known as reduplication or doubling and is done only when no quantity is defined. For example, **istri-istri** means *wives* but **tiga istri** means *three wives* and **satu istri** means *one wife*.

3 MAKING A PHONE CALL AND LEAVING A MESSAGE

Indonesians answer the phone using **halo** (*hello*), but there is no specific parting to use. If you want to *leave a message*, you simply ask if you can **titip pesan** (*entrust a message*) and start your message with **Tolong bilang …** (*Please say …*) If you're taking a message, you can assure others by saying **nanti saya sampaikan** to mean *I'll pass it on.*

Practice

1 **Put the following sentences into Indonesian.**
   a I called my older brother yesterday.
   b I will call my younger sister tomorrow.

2 **Choose the correct word.**
   a Dua *anak/anak-anak* kami tinggal di Bandung.
   b Berapa *kantor/kantor-kantor* (*offices*) mereka?

3 03.09 **Practise leaving and taking a message over the phone.**

Listening

banyak	much, many
sedikit	a few, a little

1 03.10 **Listen to the dialogue and answer the following questions.**
   a Is Wati well?
   b Is Wati married?
   c In whose house does her family live?

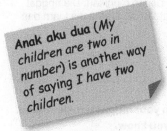
Anak aku dua (*My children are two in number*) is another way of saying *I have two children.*

2 03.11 **Listen to the recording and write down the message and who it is from in English.**

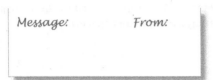

Message: From:

 3 03.12 **Read the questions below and prepare your own responses. Then, listen and respond in real time. Do this as many times as you need to for it to become second nature.**

  a Apa kabar?
  b Apa kabar keluarga Anda?
  c Apakah Anda mengerti sedikit bahasa Indonesia?

Reading and writing

 1 **Owen Rees has sent an email to his Indonesian penfriend Anisa Rusli about his family. Read the email and check the glossary if there are words you don't know.**

Halo Anisa!

Apa kabar? Apa kabar keluarga kamu?

Kabar saya dan keluarga saya baik. Saya dan orang tua saya, Peter dan Diana, tinggal di Mumbles, Wales. Ayah saya dokter. Ibu saya manajer hotel. Nenek saya, Ruby, tinggal di rumah kami juga. Saya punya dua kakak. Kakak perempuan saya, Mary, tinggal di Cardiff. Kakak laki-laki saya, Paul, belum menikah. Dia tinggal di Cardiff juga. Oh ya, Mary punya satu anak. Nama dia Liam dan saya senang bicara dengan dia.

Salam,

Owen

 2 **Imagine you are writing a letter to your Indonesian penfriend. Describe your family using what you know.**

Go further

anak tiri	*stepchild*
anak angkat	*adopted child*
bibi, tante	*aunt*
paman, om	*uncle*
sepupu	*cousin*
keponakan	*niece/nephew*

You know that in Indonesian the words **Pak** (*Sir*) and Bu (*Madam*) are short for **Bapak** and **Ibu**, respectively. When you use either of them, you are in effect addressing someone as **bapak** (*father*) and **ibu** (*mother*). In Indonesia, people don't have to be actual relatives to address each other using words that in English are reserved only for family. A young customer might address an older shopkeeper as **Kak** short for **Kakak** (*older sibling*) or **Bi** short for **Bibi** (*aunt*), for example.

The words **tante** (*aunt*) and **om** (*uncle*) are mostly used in cities and higher socioeconomic classes. They are also often used to address foreigners. Instead of using **Pak** (*Sir*) and **Bu** (*Madam*), Indonesians might address foreigners who are older than them as **Om** (*Uncle*) to mean *Sir* and **Tante** (*Aunt*) to mean *Madam*.

If you want to say that there is *much* or there are *many* of something without using numbers, use the word **banyak.**

Terima kasih banyak.

Thank you (very) much.

Dia punya banyak sepupu.

She has many cousins.

The word **sedikit** is used to mean *a few* or *a little*.

Saya bisa bicara sedikit bahasa Arab.

I can speak a little Arabic.

 1 03.13 **Read the questions below and prepare your own responses. Then, listen and respond in real time. Do this as many times as you need to for it to become second nature.**

    a Anda punya banyak saudara?

    b Anda bisa bicara bahasa Indonesia?

Test yourself

1 Use the words in the box to recreate the dialogue below.

> baik, dan, kabar, bagus, Anda, baik, apa, juga, kabar, saya

a How are you?
b I'm well. And you?
c I'm well too.
d Good!

2 Match the Indonesian to the English.

a sudah menikah   **1** *not yet married*
b belum menikah   **2** *still married*
c masih menikah   **3** *already married*

3 Put the words in English into Indonesian.

a Saya (*not yet*) pergi ke bank (*today*).
b Ibu aku (*already*) menelpon nenek kamu (*yesterday*).
c (*Tomorrow*) saya belajar.

4 Put the following words into Indonesian.

a houses
b 6 children
c 9 families

5 Complete the English translations.

a Tolong bilang saya pergi.   Please _____ I am going.
b Saya tidak mengerti.   I do not _____.
c Tolong ulang sekali lagi.   _____

SELF CHECK

	I CAN...
○	ask and answer questions about how I am and how others are
○	talk about my family
○	indicate whether I have or have not done something
○	make a phone call, and leave and take a message
○	indicate if I am (not) following the conversation

1 Give the greetings or partings that suit the time of day.
 a 9:00am
 b 1:00pm
 c 5:00pm
 d 9:00pm

2 Provide the English translations.
 a I/me/my   _____ (formal),   _____ (informal)
 b you/your   _____ (formal),   _____ (informal)
 c he/she/him/his/her   _____ (neutral)
 d we/us/our   _____ (inclusive), _____ (exclusive)
 e they, them, their   _____

3 Put the following useful expressions into Indonesian.
 a Thank you.
 b You're welcome.
 c Excuse me.
 d Until we meet again.
 e Can I speak to Ms Linda?

4 Choose the correct word to check your knowledge of questions and question words.
 a Nama kamu *siapa / apa*?
 b *Mana / Dari mana* kamu berasal?
 c *Di mana / Dari mana* kamu tinggal?
 d *Siapa / Apa* nama sekolah kamu?
 e Kamu pergi *di mana / ke mana* tadi malam?

5 Put the words in English into Indonesian.
 a (*This*) Pak Budi. Dia (*works*) di Universitas Palembang.
 b (*That*) Pak Jon. Pak Jon (*tall*). Dia (*friend*) baru Pak Budi. Dia (*English person*). Dia tahu (*Indonesian language*).
 c Linda dan Wati (*enjoy*) berselam skuba.
 d Affandi (*Linda's new neighbour*). Dia (*Indonesian person*). Dia tidak (*recognise/know*) Wati.

6 Give negative answers to the following questions.
   a Apakah dia orang Selandia Baru?
   b Mereka berlatih pencak silat tadi siang?
   c Apakah anak Anda gemuk?

7 Match the Indonesian expressions to the English.
   a Saya tidak mengerti.   1 *Please repeat once more.*
   b Tolong ulang sekali lagi.   2 *I will pass it on.*
   c Bisa titip pesan?   3 *What is your message?*
   d Apa pesan Anda?   4 *Can I leave a message?*
   e Nanti saya sampaikan.   5 *I don't understand.*

8 Check your understanding of how to talk to others about numbers and plurals by putting the following in English.
   a Berapa nomor telpon Anisa?
   b Nomor telpon aku tujuh-dua-lima-enam-nol-empat-satu-sembilan.
   c Aku punya delapan anak. Anak-anak aku tinggal di Solo.
   d Berapa saudara Anda?
   e Saudara saya tiga.

9 Use the words in the box to recreate the phrases below.

> belajar, tadi, sudah, nanti, anak, belum, pagi, masih, bekerja, punya

   a already studied earlier this morning
   b still working later
   c do not have a child yet

10 Match the statements or questions to the replies.
   a Apa kabar?   1 Tolong bilang …
   b Saya baik.   2 Kasihan!
   c Saya tidak baik.   3 Kabar baik.
   d Apa pesan kamu?   4 Bagus!

11 Suteja keeps a blog about his life in Indonesia. Read this entry about his family and answer the following questions.

Orang tua saya sekarang tinggal dengan adik laki-laki saya, Koes, di Jakarta. Nenek dan kakek saya tinggal dengan sepupu saya di Bandung. Saya tinggal di Bandung juga. Saya dan sepupu saya belajar di universitas di Bandung. Kemarin saya pergi ke rumah nenek dan kakek. Saya dan kakek bermain musik tradisional Sunda, di teras rumah mereka.

a Who lives with Suteja's parents?
b Who lives in Bandung?
c When did Suteja go to his grandparents' house?
d What did he do there?

Anda berbuat apa setiap hari?
What do you do each day?

In this unit you will learn how to:
▶ *talk about daily activities.*
▶ *use the days of the week to talk about an event or a habit.*
▶ *talk about what you and others do for a living.*
▶ *ask for and give ages.*
▶ *count people, animals, and large objects.*

CEFR (A1): *Can ask and answer questions about personal details. Can handle time.*

Daily Life

Indonesians who have an office **pekerjaan** (*job*) generally work five days a **minggu** (*week*), but exceptions are made on **Jum'at siang** (*Friday afternoon*) when Muslim men attend communal worship at the **masjid** (*mosque*). Going to and from work **setiap** (*every*) day is not a light undertaking in urban Indonesia. Commuters **mendengarkan radio** (*listen to the radio*) not only to keep up with their favourite shows but also to monitor the traffic news. Making an early start is recommended if you have appointments to keep, which can make **makan pagi** (*eating breakfast*) a hurried affair. For city-dwellers, **pulang** (*returning home*) can also take hours. Some busy professionals manage by employing a **pembantu rumah tangga** (*household servant*) to do housework such as **berbelanja** (*shopping*) for groceries and **memasak makan malam** (*cooking dinner*) for the family. The custom in humid and hot Indonesia is to **mandi** (*bathe, shower*) twice a day, once after **bangun** (*waking up*) in the morning and once in the afternoon or evening. Part of the evening may also be spent **menonton televisi** (*watching television*), a popular Indonesian pastime, or helping the children while they **membuat pekerjaan rumah** (*do homework*) before going to **tidur** (*sleep*) at night, perhaps dreaming of the **akhir minggu** (*weekend*).

How would you say *eat lunch* in Indonesian?

Vocabulary builder

04.01 Look at the words and phrases and complete the English translations. Then listen to the recording and imitate the pronunciation of the speakers.

DAYS OF THE WEEK

Senin	*Monday*
Selasa	*Tuesday*
Rabu	*Wednesday*
Kamis	*Thursday*
Jum'at	_____
Sabtu	*Saturday*
Minggu	_____

> When they're not being informal, Indonesians will say **hari Sabtu** or **hari Selasa** instead of only **Sabtu** or **Selasa**.

NUMBERS

In Indonesian, larger numbers come in groups similar to those in English, such as **belasan** (*teens*) and **puluhan** (*tens*).

10	sepuluh	20	dua puluh
11	sebelas	21	dua puluh satu
12	dua belas	22	dua puluh dua
13	tiga belas	23	dua puluh tiga
14	empat belas	24	dua puluh empat
15	lima belas	25	dua puluh lima
16	enam belas	26	dua puluh enam
17	tujuh belas	27	dua puluh tujuh
18	delapan belas	28	dua puluh delapan
19	sembilan belas	29	dua puluh sembilan
_____	tiga puluh	_____	sembilan puluh
_____	tiga puluh satu	_____	sembilan puluh sembilan

NEW EXPRESSIONS

akan	*will, going to, shall*
perusahaan	*company, corporation*

Maaf.	Sorry.
Tidak apa-apa.	*It's nothing., No worries.*
seorang	*one person (classifier)*
pegawai negeri	*government employee, civil servant*
Kapan	*When (interrogative)*
pada	*at, on, in*
umur	*age*
tahun	*year*

Conversation 1

 04.02 *Nani is talking to her colleague Frans.*

1 When is Frans' wife coming home?

Nani	Pak Frans, nanti sore kita akan pergi ke kantor perusahaan IndoTel, ya?
Frans	Hari ini hari apa?
Nani	Hari ini hari Kamis.
Frans	Oh ya. Maaf. Saya sibuk sekali minggu ini. Istri saya sedang bekerja di Lampung.
Nani	Oh, tidak apa-apa. Apa pekerjaan dia?
Frans	Dia seorang pegawai negeri.
Nani	Kapan dia pergi?
Frans	Dia pergi pada hari Selasa. Dia akan pulang pada akhir minggu.
Nani	Siapa memasak di rumah minggu ini?
Frans	Setiap hari pembantu memasak tetapi anak saya juga membantu dia di dapur.
Nani	Oh begitu. Berapa umur anak Pak Frans?
Frans	Dia berumur enam belas tahun.
Nani	Oh ya, Pak Frans sudah makan siang?
Frans	Sudah, Bu. Saya sudah makan siang.
Nani	Baiklah. Sampai nanti!
Frans	Sampai nanti!

sibuk sekali	*very busy*
tetapi	*but*
membantu	*help, assist*
dapur	*kitchen*

2 Read or listen again and answer the questions.

a What day is it?
b What does Frans' wife do for a living?
c How old is Frans' child?
d Has Frans had lunch?

3 Match the questions or statements to the replies.

a Hari ini hari apa?   **1** Dia pergi pada hari Selasa.
b Sampai nanti!   **2** Tidak apa-apa.
c Maaf.   **3** Sampai nanti!
d Kapan dia pergi?   **4** Hari ini hari Kamis.

4 Check, then cover up the replies and see if you can say them without looking at the conversation.

5 04.03 Now listen to the lines from the conversation and repeat. Then listen to Frans' lines and respond as Nani.

 # Language discovery

1 Look at the sentences from the conversation. Put the words in English into Indonesian.

a (*When*) mereka memasak? Mereka memasak (*every*) hari.
b Saya (*will*) mandi sore ini.
c Budi memasak (*dinner*). Saya (*eat dinner*) di rumah dia.
d (*How many*) umur bapak kamu?

1 WHEN

To ask about *when* something happens, Indonesians use the question word **kapan**. In reply, you use the preposition **pada** to mean *on* a certain day or *at/in* a certain time. If the event occurs regularly, use the word **setiap** to mean *each* or *every* particular day or time.

Kapan kamu berbelanja?	*When do you shop?*
Saya berbelanja pada hari Kamis.	*I shop on Thursday.*
Saya berbelanja setiap hari Kamis.	*I shop every Thursday.*

2 FUTURE ACTION

Indicating future action can be done by stating when the action will happen or by using **akan** (*will, going to*) before the verb.

Saya akan membuat pekerjaan rumah. *I will do homework.*

3 MEALS

By combining **makan** (*eat*) with a time of day, you can form words for **makan pagi** (*breakfast*), **makan siang** (*lunch*), and **makan malam** (*dinner*). You can then use the same words to say *eating breakfast*, *eating lunch*, and *eating dinner*. It is similar to how the word *lunch* in English can mean both *eating lunch* and the meal itself.

4 AGES

When asking about ages **berapa** (*how many*) is used as the answer involves a number. In reply, you can omit **tahun** (*year*) if it is clear the age is not counted in days, weeks or months.

Berapa umur dia?	*What is his age?*
Umur dia dua puluh tahun.	*His age is twenty.*

Indonesians also often use the **ber-** verbal prefix to transform the noun **umur** (*age*) into the verb **berumur** (*to be aged*).

Dia berumur dua puluh tahun. *He is aged twenty.*

 ## Practice

1 **Put the following sentences into Indonesian.**
   a When do you watch television?
   b I will come home on Friday.
   c Every Sunday I study Indonesian and cook lunch.

2 **Put the following sentences into English.**
   a Saya berbelanja besok.
   b Saya akan mendengarkan radio.
   c Saya akan belajar malam ini.

3 **Unscramble the words to make full sentences.**
   a rumah hari siang di Saya setiap makan.
   b minggu makan akhir Budi pagi pada.
   c setiap memasak malam Jon malam makan.

 4 04.04 **Practise asking and answering questions about your age and the ages of your family members.**

Pronunciation

04.05 **In Indonesian, the punctuation mark ' indicates a glottal stop. When two identical vowels are together, such as** *aa*, **there is also a glottal stop between them. A glottal stop is a sound some English speakers make in place of the letters** '*tt*' **when they pronounce the word** *butter*. **Listen to how the following words are pronounced and repeat.**

1 Jum'at

2 maaf

3 pekerjaan

4 perusahaan

Speaking

04.06 **1 Look at Nani's schedule and talk about it in Indonesian.**

Monday	shower and go to the office
Tuesday	go home, cook dinner
Wednesday	eat lunch at the office
Thursday	go to the bank, sleep
Friday	eat lunch at my parents' house
Saturday	watch television and bathe
Sunday	study English

2 Now talk about your schedule.

 Conversation 2

Nani is getting to know Linda, her new neighbour.

1 What does Linda do?

Nani	Apa pekerjaan Anda?
Linda	Saya seorang insinyur.
Nani	Wah. Di mana Anda bekerja?
Linda	Saya bekerja di sebuah perusahaan asing.
Nani	Berapa umur Anda?
Linda	Umur saya dua puluh delapan tahun.
Nani	Oh begitu. Maaf, ya? Saya harus pergi tidur.
Linda	Tidak apa-apa. Selamat tidur.

Wah	expression of awe
insinyur	*engineer*
sebuah	*one thing* (classifier)
asing	*foreign*

> Indonesians may add **ya?** to the end of sentences simply to add gentleness to their speech. Unlike the addition of *yes?* at the end of a sentence in English, it is not always a way of asking for confirmation.

2 Read or listen again and answer the following questions.
- **a** Where does Linda work?
- **b** How old is Linda?
- **c** What must Nani do?
- **d** What do you think *Selamat tidur* means?

3 Match the Indonesian to the English.

a	sebuah perusahaan	**1**	*an employee*
b	seorang pegawai	**2**	*a company*
c	seorang insinyur	**3**	*a servant*
d	seorang pembantu	**4**	*an engineer*

4 4.08 Now listen to the lines from the conversation and repeat. Be sure to pay attention to the pronunciation.

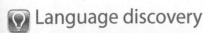

Language discovery

1 **1 Put the following sentences from the conversation into English.**

a Saya bekerja di sebuah perusahaan asing.

b Saya seorang insinyur.

1 COUNTING WITH CLASSIFIERS

In formal Indonesian, nouns are classified according to their type, shape, size, and are counted using their specific classifiers. The word **orang** (*person*), for example, is used as a classifier for people, so **dua orang insinyur** means *two engineers*. Animals are counted in **ekor** and large objects are counted in **buah**. For example, **tiga ekor burung** means *three birds* and **empat buah hotel** means *four hotels*. When there is just one of something, add the prefix **se-** to the beginning of the classifier so that you can say, for example, **seorang anak** (*a child*). In this case, **seorang** translates as *a* or *an*. In informal everyday speech, classifiers are not always used, but you should be aware of their function and try to use them when others do.

2 OCCUPATIONS

Some occupation words in Indonesia look similar to the English, such as **dokter** (*medical doctor*) and **akuntan** (*accountant*), but there are many more that don't. You may have noticed that some can be formed using the prefix **pe-** such as the word **pembantu** (*servant*) to mean a person who **membantu** (*helps*) or **pegawai** (*worker*) to mean someone who is doing **gawai** (*work*).

Practice

1 Complete the phrases using the correct classifiers.

a dua _____ kanguru

b delapan _____ perusahaan

c enam _____ pegawai

d se_____ rumah tangga

2 04.09 **Practise asking and answering questions about your occupation.**

 Listening

1 04.10 **Listen to the recording. Match the day of the week to the activity Budi did on that day.**

pada Kamis malam	on Thursday evening

a Monday
b Tuesday
c Wednesday
d Thursday
e Friday
f Saturday

g Sunday

1 went to the bank
2 cooked in the kitchen
3 went to the mosque
4 ate lunch at the office
5 called Jon
6 helped the children do their homework
7 woke up and ate breakfast at home

 2 04.11 **Read the questions below and prepare your own responses. Then, listen and respond. Do this as many times as you need to for it to become second nature.**

Berapa umur Anda?

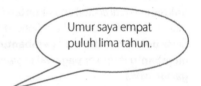

Umur saya empat puluh lima tahun.

a Hari ini hari apa?
b Kapan Anda mendengarkan radio?
c Apa pekerjaan Anda?

Reading and writing

1 Paul is currently working in Indonesia. He writes a post on an Indonesian internet forum. Read Paul's post and check the glossary if there are words you don't know.

Halo teman-teman! Saya Paul. Saya berumur tiga puluh tujuh tahun. Saya seorang guru bahasa Inggris. Saya sedang bekerja di Surabaya. Saya pergi ke kantor pada hari Senin, hari Selasa, dan hari Rabu. Saya menonton film pada Rabu malam. Pada hari Kamis saya makan siang di hotel. Pada hari Jum'at istri saya sampai di Surabaya dan kami makan malam di rumah Pak Sardi, kolega saya. Saya akan menonton televisi dan belajar bahasa Indonesia pada akhir minggu. Saya sudah mulai mengerti bahasa Indonesia tetapi saya masih harus belajar. Baiklah, saya akan tidur sekarang. Selamat malam!

2 Write a post like Paul's about your current daily life using what you know.

Go further

As you know, Indonesian revolves around root words you can build on by adding affixes. By adding **pe-** and **–an** to the word **kerja** (*to work*), you form the noun **pekerjaan** (*job*).

Here are **pekerjaan-pekerjaan** (*jobs*) you might come across:

bidan	*midwife*
ibu rumah tangga	*housewife*
ilmuwan	*scientist*
karyawan swasta	*private-sector employee*
kuli	*unskilled labourer, porter*
pekerja LSM	*NGO worker*
pelajar	*student*
pelukis	*painter*
penari	*dancer*
peneliti	*researcher*
pengajar	*educator*
perawat	*nurse*
tukang	*skilled labourer, handyman*
wartawan	*journalist*

An affix attached to the end of a word is a suffix. The suffix **–wan**, meaning someone who is knowledgeable about a particular field, is masculine. Its feminine equivalent is **–wati.**

If you are retired you can say you are a **pensiunan** (*retiree*) or that you **sudah pensiun** (*already retired*).

1 **Match the occupations to the actions. Complete the English translations of the actions.**

   a peneliti   **1** melukis   _____
   b pelajar   **2** menari   _____
   c pelukis   **3** meneliti   _____
   d penari   **4** belajar   _____

2 04.12 **Read the questions below and prepare your own reponses. Then, listen and respond in real time. Do this as many times as you need to for it to become second nature.**

   a Apa pekerjaan Isaac Newton?
   b Apa pekerjaan Florence Nightingale?

? Test yourself

1 Put the words in English into Indonesian.

   a (*When*) kamu memasak?

   b Aku mendengarkan radio (*every Tuesday night*).

   c Aku menonton televisi (*on Friday*).

   d Aku pergi ke kantor (*on Monday*).

2 Give the English for the following.

   a Saya akan membantu ibu berbelanja pada hari Sabtu.

   b Mereka mandi besok malam.

   c Saya akan membuat pekerjaan rumah saya pada hari Minggu.

3 Use the words in the box to recreate the phrases below.

> makan, makan, makan, memasak, malam, siang, pagi

   a breakfast

   b cook lunch

   c eat dinner

4 Match the Indonesian to the English.

   a Umur dia lima belas tahun.   **1** He is seventy years old.

   b Dia berumur tiga puluh tahun.   **2** He is fifteen years old.

   c Umur dia tujuh puluh tahun.   **3** She is thirty years old.

5 Put the following words into Indonesian.

   a eight children   **c** twenty four televisions

   b nineteen civil servants   **d** an NGO worker

6 Choose the correct word.

   a Apa *pekerjaan / bekerja* Anda?

   b Di mana Anda *bekerja / pekerja*?

   c Dia seorang *belajar / pelajar*.

SELF CHECK

	I CAN...
○	talk about daily activities.
○	use the days of the week to talk about an event or a habit.
○	talk about what I and others do for a living.
○	ask for and give ages.
○	count people, animals, and large objects.

5 Berapa harganya?

How much is it?

In this unit you will learn how to:

▶ *describe and ask for things.*
▶ *ask and understand how much things cost.*
▶ *pay for your shopping and receive change.*
▶ *make and understand requests.*
▶ *obtain basic information from advertisements.*

CEFR: *Can handle numbers, quantities, and cost.* **(A1)***; Can ask about things and make simple transactions in shops.* **(A2)**

Shopping

Whether you need to replace a pair of **sepatu** (*shoes*) or are looking for a **kain tradisional** (*traditional cloth*) such as the painted and patterned batik, in Indonesia there is a shopping experience to suit any budget. A medium-sized city will have at least one **mal** (*mall*) or **pusat perbelanjaan** (*shopping centre*) where you can find many shops, the **pasar swalayan** (*supermarket*), and the department store or **toserba,** which is short for **toko serba ada** (*shop that has various things*). Every community in Indonesia will also have its own traditional **pasar** (*market*), where you can buy your **belanjaan sehari-hari** (*everyday shopping*), some **barang-barang elektronik** (*electronic goods*), and **pakaian** (*clothes*). You do not need to go far, though, to buy necessities such as **pasta gigi** (*toothpaste*) or **baterai** (*batteries*) because they are commonly available at the **warung** (*street stall*), which you can find at the bottom of the neighbourhood **ruko** (*shophouse*) or at a little roadside hut. When visiting Indonesia on holiday, do seek out the specialised markets, such as the **pasar seni** (*craft and art market*), to find a unique **oleh-oleh** (*souvenir*). With some Indonesian rupiah in hand, you can **beli** (*buy*) just about anything you **suka** (*like*) in Indonesia.

 How would you say *batik shop* in Indonesian?

Vocabulary builder

05.01 Look at the words and phrases and complete the English translations. Then listen to the recording and imitate the pronunciation of the speakers.

SHOPPING

harga	*price, value*
warna	*colour*
ukuran	*size*
pas	*to fit, accurate, exactly*
kasir	*cashier, till (coll.)*
uang	*money (also notes and coins)*
uang kembalian	*change*
uang tunai	*cash*
kartu kredit	_____
diskon	_____

ADJECTIVES

mahal	*expensive*
murah	*cheap*
besar	*large*
kecil	*small*
panjang	*long*
pendek	*short*

NEW EXPRESSIONS

cari	*look for, search for*
boleh	*may, to be allowed to*
lihat	*see, look at*
yang	*that, which, that which*
Yang mana?	*Which one/ones?*
ada	*there is/are, has/have, to be available*
coba	*try*
tunggu sebentar	*wait a moment*
ambil	*take*
bayar	*pay*
kalau	*if, when*
mau	*want*
Kembali.	*(Thanks) in return./You're welcome.*

NUMBERS

In Indonesian, the **se-** prefix often takes the place of **satu** (*one*).

100	**seratus**	500	**lima ratus**
1000	**seribu**	5000	**lima ribu**
10,000	**sepuluh ribu**	50,000	**lima puluh ribu**
100,000	**seratus ribu**	500,000	**lima ratus ribu**
1,000,000,000	**sejuta** *or* **satu juta**	5,000,000,000	**lima juta**

Prices of everyday goods in Indonesian rupiah run into the tens and hundreds of thousands. Being familiar with large numbers is a necessity, especially if you plan to shop at markets or road stalls where many items do not have a price sticker.

QUALIFIERS

kurang	*not quite, less*
lebih	*more*
paling	*most*
terlalu	*too, overly*

COLOURS

merah	*red*	**biru**	*blue*
kuning	*yellow*	**hijau**	*green*
putih	*white*	**hitam**	*black*
coklat	*brown*	**abu-abu**	*grey*

When referring to a colour, Indonesians will say, for example, **warna putih** instead of only **putih** (*white*).

CLOTHING

kaos	*t-shirt*	**kemeja**	*shirt*
celana	*trousers*	**rok**	*skirt*
jas	*blazer, coat*	**dasi**	*tie*
baju dalam	*underclothes*	**topi**	*hat*
kaos kaki	*socks*	**sendal**	*sandals*

Remember, you don't need to pluralise items that usually come in pairs, such as **sendal** (*sandals*), unless you're talking about many pairs of them.

 05.02 Listen to the numbers and useful words and imitate the pronunciation of the speakers.

Conversation 1

 05.03 *Tono is a teenager shopping at a department store and Mokhtar is a sales attendant who is helping him.*

1 How much are the black shoes?

Mokhtar	Kamu cari apa?
Tono	Aku cari sepatu. Aku boleh lihat yang itu?
Mokhtar	Yang mana?
Tono	Yang biru.

[Mokhtar gives Tono the shoes Tono pointed to.]

Tono	Berapa harganya?
Mokhtar	Harganya tiga ratus ribu rupiah.
Tono	Itu terlalu mahal. Ada sepatu yang lebih murah?
Mokhtar	Ada. Yang hitam dua ratus ribu rupiah.
Tono	Yang hitam sepatu yang paling murah?
Mokhtar	Ya. Yang paling murah. Cobalah.

[Tono tries on the shoes.]

Tono	Yang ini kurang pas. Yang ini terlalu kecil.
Mokhtar	Berapa ukuranmu?
Tono	Ukuranku empat puluh satu.
Mokhtar	Tolong tunggu sebentar. Saya cari ukuranmu.

[Mokhtar returns with the shoes and Tono tries them on.]

Tono	Ya. Yang ini pas. Aku ambil yang ini.
Mokhtar	Silakan bayar di kasir.
Tono	Aku boleh bayar dengan kartu kredit?
Mokhtar	Boleh, tetapi hari ini kalau kamu bayar tunai, ada diskon sepuluh persen.

2 Find the expressions in the conversation that mean:
a Try (them on). _____
b Please wait a moment. _____
c Please pay at the till. _____

3 Read or listen again and answer the questions.
a What colour are the cheapest shoes?
b What is Tono's shoe size?
c How can Tono qualify for the ten percent discount?

4 05.04 Now listen to the lines from the conversation and repeat. Be sure to pay attention to the pronunciation.

Language discovery

1 Look at the sentences from the conversation. Put the words in English into Indonesian.

   a Aku boleh lihat (*those ones*)? Yang mana? (*The blue ones.*)
   b (*Please*) tunggu sebentar. (*Please*) bayar di kasir.
   c Ada (*cheaper shoes*)?
   d Berapa (*your size*)? (*My size*) empat puluh satu.
   e Berapa (*its price*)?

1 SINGLING OUT ITEMS USING *YANG*

To single out items, you can use the word **yang** (*that, which*) in several ways. When you say **topi yang biru**, you're talking about *the hat that is blue* and not any other hat. You don't always need to use the noun **topi** (*hat*) either. You can simply say **yang biru** (*the blue one*). Similarly, instead of saying **topi yang itu** (*that hat*), you can say **yang itu** (*that one*). If you need clarification when others are pointing at items, ask **Yang mana?** (*Which one?*).

Note that since in the Indonesian **yang ini** (*this one*) does not actually describe the number of items present, it can also mean *these ones*. Similarly, **yang biru** can be either *the blue one* or *the blue ones*.

2 MAKING REQUESTS OR SUGGESTIONS

When requesting or suggesting an action, you can simply use the verb. Sometimes **–lah** is added to the verb for emphasis.

Coba sepatu itu. Cobalah sepatu itu.

Try (on) those shoes. Do try (on) those shoes.

To be more polite, you can use the word **silakan** (*please, go ahead*) when the action will benefit the person to whom the action is suggested. However, you should use the word **tolong** (*please, help*) when the action you request will be mutually beneficial or beneficial to you.

Silakan bayar di kasir.

Please (for your convenience) pay at the till.

Tolong tunggu sebentar. Saya cari ukuranmu.

Please wait a moment (for me). I will look for your size.

3 QUALIFYING DESCRIPTIONS

When you want to describe something as being **terlalu kecil** (*too small*) or **kurang kecil** (*not small enough*), or if you want to say you are looking for something **lebih kecil** (*smaller*) or for **paling kecil** (*the smallest*) of its kind, place the qualifier before the adjective.

Ini kecil. Ini kurang kecil. Ini terlalu kecil.

This is small. This is not small enough. This is too small.

The word **yang** is necessary when you're describing a noun, for example **sepatu yang lebih murah** (*the cheaper shoes*). When the noun, in this case **sepatu** (*shoes*), is already known, you can simply say **yang lebih murah** to mean *the cheaper ones*.

4 ATTACHED POSSESSIVE PRONOUNS

In Indonesian, possessive pronouns such as **aku** (*my*), **kamu** (*your*), **dia** (*his/her*), and **mereka** (*their*) are often attached to the noun in the form of suffixes such as **–ku** (*my*), **-mu** (*your*), and **–nya** (*his/her, their*).

Therefore, **ukuran aku** becomes **ukuranku** (*my size*), **ukuran kamu** becomes **ukuranmu** (*your size*) and **ukuran dia** or **ukuran mereka** becomes **ukurannya** (*his/her size, their size*). In this way, an inanimate object such as an item for sale can also be treated as possessive, for example, **harganya** (*its price*).

When talking about a noun phrase, such as **ukuran celana** (*trouser size*), you attach the pronoun to the end of the phrase.

Berapa ukuran celanamu?

What is your trouser size?

5 PRICE

When you ask how much something is, you are asking for **harganya** (*its price*). Since the answer involves a number, you should use the question word **berapa** (*how many*). In everyday speech it is not always necessary to include the currency.

Berapa harganya? Harganya lima puluh ribu rupiah.

What is its price? Its price is fifty thousand rupiah.

Berapa harga yang itu? Sepuluh ribu.

What is that one's price? Ten thousand.

Practice

1 **Put the following sentences into Indonesian.**
   a Which one is the cheapest one?
   b I'm taking this one.

2 **Put the words in English into Indonesian.**
   a (*Please, help*) cari ukuran saya.
   b (*Please, go ahead*) bayar dengan kartu kredit.

3 **Put the following sentences into English.**
   a Celana pendek itu terlalu besar.
   b Kaos kaki ini kurang panjang.

4 **Replace the pronouns with attached pronouns.**
   a Ukuran kemeja saya enam belas.
   b Rok dia hijau dan rok kamu abu-abu.

5 05.05 **Practise asking and telling others about how much things cost in Indonesian rupiah.**

 Pronunciation

 05.06 **The Indonesian consonant *ny* is used frequently and unlike in English, it can also be found at the beginning of words and immediately after other consonants. Listen to how the following words are pronounced and repeat.**

> Try to pronounce the English words '*canyon*' and '*onion*' while paying attention to the ny sound you are making.

1 harganya
2 ukurannya
3 pakaiannya
4 nyamuk

Speaking

 05.07 **Read the questions below and prepare your own responses. Then, listen and respond. Do this as many times as you need to for it to become second nature.**

a Di mana kamu berbelanja?

b Kalau di Indonesia, kamu berbelanja di ruko?

c Berapa ukuranmu?

 Conversation 2

05.08 *Linda goes to a street stall to shop.*

Linda	Selamat siang, Pak.
Penjual	Selamat siang. Ibu mau beli apa?
Linda	Saya mau beli sikat gigi, Pak.
Penjual	Ibu suka warna apa?
Linda	Saya suka warna hijau muda dan warna biru tua.

[The vendor shows Linda the goods.]

Penjual	Ini, Bu. Ibu mau yang mana?
Linda	Saya ambil yang biru tua. Berapa harganya?
Penjual	Sepuluh ribu saja. Ibu mau beli pasta gigi juga?
Linda	Tidak. Terima kasih. Saya tidak mau beli pasta gigi hari ini.
Penjual	Oh ya. Tidak apa-apa.
Linda	Saya tidak ada uang pas. Saya ada uang dua puluh ribu saja. Ada uang kembalian?
Penjual	Ada. Ini kembalian Ibu. Sepuluh ribu pas.
Linda	Terima kasih.
Penjual	Kembali.

penjual	vendor, seller
sikat	brush
suka	like (v.)
saja	merely, only

1 What does Linda want to buy?

> The response **kembali** is short for **terima kasih kembali** meaning *thank you in return.*

2 Match the Indonesian to the English.

a yang biru tua   **1** *ten thousand exactly*
b uang dua puluh ribu   **2** *the dark blue one*
c sepuluh ribu pas   **3** *change*
d uang kembalian   **4** *a twenty-thousand rupiah note*

3 Check, then cover up your answers and see if you can say them without looking at the conversation.

4 Read or listen again and answer the following questions.
a What colours did Linda say she likes?
b What else did the stall vendor offer Linda?
c What was the denomination of the bill that Linda used to pay?
d Did the vendor have change?

5 05.09 Now listen to the lines from the conversation and repeat. Then listen to the vendor's lines and respond as Linda.

 # Language discovery

1 Look at the sentences from the conversation. Put the words in English into Indonesian.
a Ibu (*want to buy*) apa?
b Saya (*have*) uang dua puluh ribu. (*Is there*) uang kembalian?
c Saya suka warna (*light green*) dan (*deep blue*).

1 VERB COMBINATIONS

When you need to combine verbs to say, for example, that you *want to buy* something, you simply put **mau** (*want*) and **beli** (*buy*) together to make **mau beli.** When you negate it, you should place **tidak** before the combination.

2 THE VERB *ADA*

The verb **ada** can mean *there is* or *here are*.

Ada toko komputer di mal itu.   *There is a computer shop in that shopping mall.*

Colloquially, you can also use it to mean *to have*.

Saya ada uang pas.   *I have exact change.*

It can also mean *to be available*.

Dasi yang biru masih ada.   *The blue tie is still available.*

3 DARKER AND LIGHTER COLOURS

Consider how the colour of leaves grows into a deeper green as a plant ages throughout the growing season. When you want to talk about a darker version of a colour, you can use the word **tua** (*old*) to mean *dark* or *deep* so that, for example, **merah tua** is *dark red* or *deep red*. To talk about a lighter version of a colour, you can use the word **muda** (*young*) to mean *light* so that, for example, **merah muda** is *light red* or *pink*.

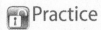 Practice

1 **Put the words in English into Indonesian.**
   a Saya (*may see*) jas (*that is red*)?
   b Dia (*want to go*) ke (*street stall*) dan beli baterai.

2 **Put the following sentences into English.**
   a Maaf. Saya tidak ada uang pas.
   b Ponsel itu masih ada, Pak, dan ada diskon dua puluh persen!

 3   05.10 **Practise describing the colours of things.**

> Sendal saya putih.
> Kaos saya abu-abu muda. ...

 Listening

dijual	*for sale (lit. being sold)*
hubungi	*contact (v.)*
sepasang	*a pair of*
setengah	*half*

1 05.11 **Maya is looking at the classifieds in the paper whilst eating breakfast with her husband Slamet. Listen to the dialogue and answer the following questions.**
   a Is the house large or small?
   b Why are they interested in the house?
   c How much is the house?

The word **dijual** (to be sold) comes from the prefix **di-** and the word **jual** (to sell). In Indonesia, it is the most common way to title for sale listings.

2 05.12 **Benny is at the market. Listen to the dialogue and complete the sentences in the story.**

Benny mau membeli sepasang sendal _____. Ukurannya _____. _____ ukurannya di pasar. Sekarang dia akan coba pergi ke _____ di mana sendal itu juga _____. Kalau tidak ada juga di _____, Benny harus pergi ke _____.

 Reading and writing

1 Whose advertisement has Amelia responded to?

Social media **iklan** (advertisement) is a popular solution for Indonesian small businesses and home industries that once relied largely on word-of-mouth promotion.

twitter

Home Profile Find People Setings Helps Sign Out

DIJUAL sepatu anak-anak. Warna-warna kuning, hijau, dan merah masih ada. Murah dan bagus! Hubungi Ira 016.726.0924

DIJUAL murah! Barang-barang elektronik: komputer, HP, telepon, baterai murah! Hubungi Santoso 0811.3038.7712

Halo. Saya lihat iklan Anda. Saya mau sepasang sepatu anak-anak yang kuning dan sepasang yang merah. Ukuran anak saya 3 1/2. Kalau ukuran dan warna itu masih ada, tolong hubungi saya di 0811.6690.0925. Amelia

2 Imagine you are responding to one of the above advertisements. Write your reply. Don't forget to give your contact details.

Go further

In Indonesian, composing large numbers is done in a similar way to how it is done in English. You start with the largest group, for example the **jutaan** (*millions*), and move to the second largest, for example the **ribuan** (*thousands*), then to the **ratusan** (*hundreds*) and to the tens, and so on.

> 2015 = 2,000 + 15
> **dua ribu lima belas**
> two thousand (and) fifteen
> 23,450 = 23,000 + 400 + 50
> **dua puluh tiga ribu empat ratus lima puluh**
> twenty three thousand, four hundred (and) fifty
> 2,630,500 = 2,000,000 + 630,000 + 500
> **dua juta enam ratus tiga puluh ribu lima ratus**
> two million, six hundred (and) thirty thousand, (and) five hundred

1 **Put the following amounts of money into Indonesian.**
   a 950 rupiah
   b 4,200 rupiah
   c 12,900 rupiah
   d 750,000 rupiah
   e 1,625,000 rupiah

2 **Match the Indonesian to the English.**

a	apotek	1	*electronics shop*
b	toko elektronik	2	*copy shop*
c	pasar seni	3	*bookshop*
d	toko fotokopi	4	*craft and art market*
e	toko buku	5	*pharmacy*

3 05.13 **Read the questions below and prepare your own responses. Then, listen and respond in real time. Do this as many times as you need to for it to become second nature.**
   a Di mana Anda mau membeli oleh-oleh dari Indonesia?
   b Anda paling suka warna apa?
   c Berapa harga belanjaan sehari-hari Anda?
   d Di kota Anda, di mana aspirin dijual?

? Test yourself

1 Put the words in English into Indonesian.
   a *(Which one)* kamu mau lihat?
   b Saya boleh lihat *(that one)*?
   c Saya mau membeli *(this one)*.

2 Complete the sentences to make polite requests.
   a _____ bayar dengan uang pas. *(for your/mutual benefit)*
   b _____ coba yang Anda suka. *(for the other person's benefit)*

3 Match the Indonesian to the English.
   a kurang murah   **1** *too long*
   b paling besar   **2** *not cheap enough*
   c terlalu panjang   **3** *largest*

4 Put the following sentences into English.
   a Ini bukan ukuranku.
   b Ukuranmu sembilan setengah.
   c Ukurannya terlalu kecil.

5 Unscramble the words to make full sentences.
   a coklat yang harga pendek Berapa rok ?
   b ratus puluh dua Harganya rupiah ribu dua.

6 Choose the correct phrase.
   a Saya *mau ke pergi / mau pergi* ke pasar seni.
   b Saya *boleh coba / boleh ke coba* celana panjang itu?

7 Insert the word **ada** into the sentences to correct them.
   a Tidak baju dalam di toko ini.
   b Kami kain-kain tradisional.

8 Choose the correct English translation.
   a merah muda   *pink / dark red*
   b hijau tua   *light green / dark green*

SELF CHECK

	I CAN ...
○	describe and ask for things
○	ask and understand how much things cost.
○	pay for my shopping and receive change.
○	make and understand requests.
○	obtain basic information from advertisements.

6 *Anda menginap di mana?*
Where are you staying?

In this unit you will learn how to:
▶ *talk about types of accommodation.*
▶ *express your preferences and make reservations.*
▶ *use the months of the year to talk about dates.*
▶ *ask for and give addresses.*
▶ *ask for, give, and understand Indonesian spelling.*

CEFR: *Can fill in forms of personal details of self or others.* **(A1)**; *Can explain what he likes or dislikes.* **(A2)**

Accommodation

Finding **akomodasi** (*accommodation*) in Indonesia that offers what you **perlu** (*need*) and like, such as **AC** (*air conditioning*) or internet access, will be easy. If you prefer staying in hotels, you can choose a **hotel berbintang** (*star-rated hotel*) or a **hotel melati** (*jasmine-rated hotel*), where your room will come with fewer or more modest **fasilitas** (*amenities*). With Indonesia being a tropical country, not all accommodations feature **air panas** (*hot water*). Bathrooms may also come with only a **bak mandi** (*bathtub*) and a **gayung** (*dipper*) that you use to scoop water out of the tub to wash yourself instead of a **pancuran mandi** (*shower*). In smaller cities, you can **menginap** (*stay overnight*) at the more intimate and often family-run **losmen** (*guesthouse*). If you find yourself in a town or **desa** (*village*) where there is no **penginapan** (*commercially-run accommodation*), you're likely to meet locals who will want to host you as their **tamu** (*guest*). When staying for more than a **bulan** (*month*), you can consider **menyewa** (*renting*) a residence of your own or a **kamar kos** (*bedsit*), where you would live with an Indonesian family or in a specially built **rumah kos** (*boarding house*), as Indonesian students and young professionals often do.

How would you say *I need hot water amenities* in Indonesian?

Vocabulary builder

06.01 Look at the words and phrases and complete the English translations. Then listen to the recording and imitate the pronunciation of the speakers.

ACCOMMODATION

kamar singel	single room
kamar dobel	_____ room
kamar mandi	bathroom
kamar mandi di dalam	en-suite bathroom
tarif	rate, fee, fare
per malam, semalam	_____ a night
memesan	book (v.), order (v.)
reservasi, pemesanan	reservation
konfirmasi	_____

MONTHS OF THE YEAR

Januari	January
Februari	February
Maret	March
April	April
Mei	May
Juni	June
Juli	July
Agustus	August
September	September
Oktober	October
November, Nopember	November
Desember	December

NEW EXPRESSIONS

tanggal	date
untuk	for, for the purpose of
lebih ... daripada ...	more ... than ...
atau	or
dalam	inside, within, in
hanya	only
lahir	to be born

 Conversation 1

06.02 *Linda calls a guesthouse to book a room.*

1 When does Linda want to stay at the guesthouse?

> The pronunciation of **AC** is a mix of English and Indonesian.

Shinta	Halo. Losmen Ratu. Ini Shinta. Bisa saya bantu?
Linda	Halo. Ini Linda Curtis. Saya mencari akomodasi untuk akhir bulan Mei.
Shinta	Pada tanggal berapa Anda mau menginap?
Linda	Saya mau menginap dari tanggal tiga puluh Mei sampai tanggal dua Juni. Saya perlu satu kamar.
Shinta	Kami ada kamar kosong untuk tanggal-tanggal tersebut. Untuk berapa orang tamu?
Linda	Untuk dua orang tamu. Saya dan suami saya.
Shinta	Anda mau kamar ber-AC atau tanpa AC?
Linda	Saya lebih suka kamar ber-AC daripada kamar tanpa AC. Saya kurang suka tidur tanpa AC.
Shinta	Kami ada satu kamar dobel ber-AC dengan kamar mandi di dalam.
Linda	Ada pancuran mandi di dalam kamar mandinya?
Shinta	Maaf. Tidak ada. Hanya ada bak mandi.
Linda	Tidak apa-apa. Apakah ada fasilitas internet?
Shinta	Ya. Ada.
Linda	Berapa tarif kamar per malam?
Shinta	Tarifnya semalam seratus tiga puluh ribu rupiah.
Linda	Baiklah. Saya mau memesan kamar itu.

mencari	*look for, search for*
kosong	*empty*
tersebut	*mentioned, said*
tanpa	*without, lacking*

2 Find the expressions in the conversation that mean:

  a Can I help (you)? _____
  b There isn't. _____
  c What is the room rate per night? _____

3 **Read or listen again and answer the questions.**
   a Who will be travelling with Linda?
   b What are the features of the bathroom?
   c How much does the room cost?

4 06.03 **Now listen to the lines from the conversation and repeat. Be sure to pay attention to the pronunciation.**

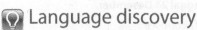 # Language discovery

1 **Look at the sentences from the conversation. Put the words in English into Indonesian.**
   a Saya (*prefer*) hotel berbintang (*instead of*) hotel melati.
   b Saya (*do not quite*) suka mandi dengan gayung.
   c *Dari* (*what date*) dia menginap? Dari (*the 30th of May*).

1 EXPRESSING PREFERENCE

You've seen the qualifier **lebih** (*more*) used on its own, but it can also be used with **daripada** (*than*) to explicitly compare one thing with another.

Kamar dobel lebih mahal daripada kamar singel.

A double room is more expensive than a single room.

Using **lebih** (*more*) to say you **suka** (*like*) something more than another thing is an easy way to express your preference.

Saya lebih suka bulan Juni daripada bulan Juli.

I like June more than I like July. I prefer June instead of July.

Saya lebih suka bulan Oktober.   *I prefer October.*

2 EXPRESSING DISLIKE

When you want to show dislike, you combine the verb **suka** (*like*) with **tidak** (*not*) to say you **tidak suka** (*do not like*) something. However, Indonesians often prefer to say they merely **kurang suka** (*do not quite like*) something, which is more polite.

Saya kurang suka menginap di rumah mereka.

I do not quite like staying overnight at their house.

3 THE DATE

When stating a *date*, you'll need to preface it with the word **tanggal**. You should use **pada** when an event happens *on* a particular date and **berapa** (*how many*) as a question word.

Saya menginap di kota Bogor pada tanggal 31 Mei.

I stayed overnight in the city of Bogor on the 31st of May.

Hari ini tanggal berapa? Hari ini tanggal 24 Desember.

What date is it today? Today is the 24th of December.

As in English, the year is placed at the end of the date. For example, **tanggal 24 Desember 2016**. You should say **tahun 2016** if you need to talk about *the year 2016* on its own.

 Practice

1 Put the following sentences into Indonesian.
   a They prefer a star-rated hotel instead of a guesthouse.
   b I prefer a bathroom with hot water amenities.
   c She prefers renting a bedsit.

2 Put the following sentences into English.
   a Maaf. Saya kurang suka kamar ini.
   b Mereka tidak suka hotel itu.
   c Saya kurang suka tinggal di rumah kos.

 06.04 **3 Practise asking and telling people what date it is today.**

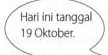

Hari ini tanggal berapa?

Hari ini tanggal 19 Oktober.

 Pronunciation

 06.05 **Listen to how the alphabet is pronounced so you can spell it as an Indonesian speaker. Do this as many times as you need to for it to become second nature.**

Speaking

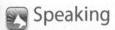 **06.06 Look at the schedule, read the questions, and make the reservations. Then, listen and respond in real time.**

Di mana Anda mau menginap?

Kapan Anda mau menginap?

Anda perlu berapa kamar?

Untuk berapa orang tamu?

 ## Conversation 2

 06.07 Shinta and Linda are still on the phone while Shinta makes Linda's reservation at the guesthouse.

1 What are the details of Linda's reservation?

Shinta	Anda bisa mengeja nama Anda?
Linda	Ya. L—I—N—D—A C—U—R—T—I—S.
Shinta	Terima kasih. Ya, sekarang Ibu Linda sudah ada reservasi di losmen kami dari tanggal tiga puluh Mei sampai tanggal dua Juni. Kamar dobel ber-AC dengan kamar mandi di dalam dan fasilitas internet. Betul, Bu?
Linda	Betul. Terima kasih.
Shinta	Kembali. Ibu sudah ada alamat kami?
Linda	Belum. Di mana alamatnya?
Shinta	Alamatnya Jalan Lumumba nomor tiga puluh lima.
Linda	Shinta bisa mengeja nama jalannya?
Shinta	Bisa. L—U—M—U—M—B—A.
Linda	Terima kasih, Shinta.

mengeja	spell (v.)
betul	correct
alamat	address
Jalan	Street, Road

> Recall that when someone is speaking to you, words such as **Anda** (*you, your*) may be replaced by your name.

2 Match the questions or statements to the replies.

a	Betul, Bu?	**1**	Alamatnya Jalan Lumumba.
b	Di mana alamatnya?	**2**	Belum.
c	Terima kasih.	**3**	Betul.
d	d Ibu sudah ada alamatnya?	**4**	Kembali.

3 Check, then cover up your answers and see if you can say them without looking at the conversation.

4 Read or listen again and answer the following questions.
    a What did Shinta ask Linda to do?
    b Did Linda have the address of the guesthouse?
    c What is the address?

5 06.08 Now listen to the lines from the conversation and repeat. Then listen to Linda's lines and respond as Shinta.

 Language discovery

1 Refer to the conversation and match the Indonesian to the English.
    a alamatnya   **1** the street name
    b nama jalannya   **2** the address

2 Unscramble the words to make full sentences using the conversation as a model.
    a alamatnya? mana Di
    b Lumumba nomor puluh Jalan Alamatnya lima tiga.

1 THE –NYA SUFFIX ACTING AS *THE*

When discussing a particular thing or person, Indonesians add the suffix –**nya** to the noun instead of continually describing *the* thing or person they are talking about. In Conversation 2, it was understood that **alamatnya** (*the address*) was that of the guesthouse. When Linda asked Shinta to spell **nama jalannya** (*the street name*), it was understood that Linda was referring to the street in the address Shinta just gave her.

2 ASKING FOR AND GIVING AN ADDRESS

An address is treated as a location in Indonesian so you need to use **di mana** (*where*) instead of the question word **apa** when asking someone

what the address is. In an Indonesian address, the street name comes
before the house number.

Di mana alamatmu? *What is your address?*

Alamatku Jalan Pattimura nomor dua belas.

My address is Street Pattimura No. 12.

 Practice

1 **Put the following questions into Indonesian using the –nya suffix.**
   a Where is the bathroom?
   b Who is the guest?
   c What is the address?

 2 06.09 **Practise asking and answering questions about your address.**

> Di mana
> alamat Anda?

> Alamat saya Jalan
> Downshire nomor
> dua belas.

 Listening

memberikan ... kepada ...	give (something) to (someone)
selama	for a duration of
termasuk	included

1 06.10 **Listen to the voicemail message left for Jon Curtis by
   a Hotel Ambarawa staff member and answer the following
   questions.**
   a When is Jon going to stay at Hotel Ambarawa?
   b How many nights is the reservation for?
   c How much is the room per night in dollars?
   d What is included in the price of the room?

2 06.11 **Listen to the announcement. Write down the dates in
   Indonesian, matching them with the destinations.**

> Surabaya   Ambon   Manado
> Semarang   Medan   Batam
> Padang   Jakarta   Makassar

Reading and writing

1 Read the booking confirmation letter.

Hotel Arjuna

Kepada YTH Ibu Marni

JL Kintamani No. 14, Depok 16424

Tel. (021)650-0592

Dengan ini kami memberikan konfirmasi pemesanan kamar Anda. Anda menginap selama empat malam dari tanggal 3 Mei. Satu kamar dobel tanpa AC dengan kamar mandi di dalam. Tarif kamar semalam enam puluh dolar, termasuk makan pagi.

Hormat saya,

Irwan Sudibyo

YTH is short for **Yang Terhormat** (*Whom is most respected*), a standard way of addressing others in Indonesian business correspondence.

2 Complete the hotel registration form for Marni. Then, practise completing the form with your own details.

Hotel Arjuna	
a Nama Tamu: _____	**b** _____ Lahir: 17/6/1971
c Alamat: _____	**d** Kota: _____
e Kode Pos: _____	**f** No. Telepon: _____

Go further

When choosing your accommodation, you may have particular **keperluan-keperluan** (*needs*). Here are some accommodation features that you may come across.

1 **Match the Indonesian to the English.**

   a kamar bebas rokok   **1** *work desk*

   b tempat tidur ekstra   **2** *iron and ironing board*

   c ranjang bayi   **3** *extra bed*

   d brankas   **4** *tea and coffee maker*

   e setrika dan papan setrika   **5** *hair dryer*

   f meja kerja   **6** *smoke-free room*

   g pembuat teh dan kopi   **7** *safe*

   h pengering rambut   **8** *baby cot*

Earlier, you discovered how the word **dalam** can be used with a currency to mean *in* that currency. It can also be used with a language to mean *in* that language. Whenever you need help, you can ask what something means **dalam bahasa Inggris** (*in English*) or **dalam bahasa Indonesia** (*in Indonesian*).

Apa arti 'kolam renang' dalam bahasa Inggris?

What is the meaning of 'kolam renang' in English?

Artinya 'swimming pool'.   *Its meaning is 'swimming pool'.*

---

2 06.12 **Put the following dialogue into Indonesian except for the words in quotations. Then, listen to Jon's lines and respond as if you were Budi.**

Jon	*What is the meaning of 'internet gratis' in English?*
Budi	*Its meaning is 'free internet'.*
Jon	*What is the meaning of 'unlimited wifi' in Indonesian?*
Budi	*Its meaning is 'koneksi wifi tanpa batas'.*

3 06.13 **Read the questions below and prepare responses that are true for you. Then, listen and respond in real time. Do this as many times as you need to for it to become second nature.**

Di Indonesia, Anda menginap di mana?

Apa keperluan Anda dan keluarga Anda?

Apakah Anda akan mencari kamar kos di Indonesia?

❓ Test yourself

1 Unscramble the words to make full sentences.
   a Dia AC lebih kamar suka tanpa .
   b hotel suka Budi menginap lebih berbintang di.
   c Mereka singel suka kamar dobel kamar daripada lebih.

2 Insert the word **kurang** into the sentences to negate them.
   a Saya suka menginap di penginapan.
   b Aku suka menyewa kamar kos.
   c Mereka suka belajar pada akhir minggu.

3 Put the words in English into Indonesian.
   a Hari ini (*what date*)?
   b Saya menginap di hotel melati (*on the 17th of January*).
   c Besok (*the 23rd of September*).

4 Put the following questions into English.
   a Di mana hotelnya?
   b Berapa tarif kamarnya per malam?
   c Berapa nomor teleponnya?

5 Correct the underlined words.
   a <u>Apa</u> alamat Anda?
   b Anda bisa memberikan alamatnya <u>ke</u> saya?
   c Alamatnya <u>Malam</u> Rusa No. 81.

SELF CHECK	
I CAN ...	
○	talk about types of accommodation.
○	express my preferences and make reservations.
○	use the months of the year to talk about dates.
○	ask for and give addresses.
○	ask for, give, and understand Indonesian spelling.

1 Match the Indonesian to the English.

a	Kamis	1	*Monday*
b	Minggu	2	*Friday*
c	hari	3	*Thursday*
d	Jum'at	4	*day*
e	Selasa	5	*Saturday*
f	Senin	6	*Tuesday*
g	Sabtu	7	*week*
h	minggu	8	*Sunday*

2 Everyday Indonesian questions are very simple. Give the questions that match the answers.

a Umur aku lima tahun.

b Aku mandi tadi pagi dan tadi sore.

c Aku cari kemeja putih.

d Aku mau beli baterai.

e Ukuranku empat setengah.

f Harganya tiga puluh delapan ribu rupiah.

g Yang panjang.

h Aku menginap di hotel berbintang.

i Alamatnya Jalan Mawar nomor dua.

3 Put the following everyday expressions into Indonesian.

a Sleep well.

b Please pay at the till (for your convenience).

c Please wait a moment.

d Do buy (it).

e Today is Wednesday, the 8th of August.

4 Help Jon complete his Indonesian blog entry by putting the words in English into Indonesian.

> **Blog**   Add post
>
> Kemarin aku (*returned home*) pada malam hari dan (*went to sleep*) tanpa (*having dinner*) atau (*watching television*). Tadi pagi, aku (*woke up*), (*bathed*), dan pergi ke kantor. Aku tidak (*have breakfast*). Istri adikku berkata, 'Jon, bulan ini kamu terlalu (*busy*)!' Aku (*will*) pergi ke Bali (*at the weekend*) dan berselancar. Aku mau pergi ke Inggris (*in May*).

5 Give the following in English.
  a tujuh belas tahun
  b sepuluh orang
  c sembilan bulan
  d tahun delapan ratus enam
  e satu juta lima ratus ribu rupiah

6 Anisa has written an email to her Welsh penfriend Owen to tell him about her family's trip to a shopping mall. Read the email and answer the following questions.

> Halo Owen!
>
> Keluargaku berbelanja di mal kemarin. Bapakku beli radio baru. Warna radio itu coklat tua. Ibuku beli rok dan jas untuk pergi ke kantor. Ibu juga beli kaos-kaos merah dan kuning muda untuk adik-adikku. Aku beli baterai HP baru dan sepasang sendal biru tua. Aku kurang suka warna biru tua. Aku lebih suka warna abu-abu tetapi yang abu-abu tidak ada di mal. Apakah ada mal di Wales? Keluarga kamu berbelanja di mana?
>
> Salam,
>
> Anisa

  a Who bought the new radio?
  b What work clothes did Anisa's mother buy?
  c What are the colours of the t-shirts?
  d What did Anisa buy?
  e Why did she not buy the grey ones?

7 Siti is counting what she can see out of her window. Help her choose the correct classifiers.

  a tiga *pasang / ekor* sepatu   three pairs of shoes
  b enam *orang / ekor* burung   six birds
  c dua *orang / ekor* ilmuwan   two scientists
  d empat *pasang / buah* rumah   four houses

8 Use the contents of the box to complete the sentences so that they match the English translations.

silakan,   -lah,   tolong

  a cari losmen   Do look for a guesthouse.
  b bantu saya   Please help me.
  c menginap di rumah kami   Please stay at our house.

9 Match the questions or statements to the replies.

  a Maaf.   **1** Maaf. Yang ini tidak dijual.
  b Terima kasih.   **2** Sampai nanti!
  c Yang mana lebih murah?   **3** Tidak apa-apa.
  d Sampai nanti!   **4** Artinya *'guest'*.
  e Apa arti 'tamu'?   **5** Yang ini lebih murah.
  f f Aku boleh lihat yang itu?   **6** Terima kasih kembali.

10 Unscramble the words to make full sentences.

  a pada malam Maret kamar Berapa per tarif bulan?
  b dobel memesan Saya kamar mau.
  c reservasi Anda kami di ada hotel sudah?

11 Bima recently talked to an oral historian about his daily life and his household. Read the historian's transcript and answer the following questions.

> Saya karyawan di sebuah perusahaan asing. Istri saya seorang ibu rumah tangga. Dia lebih suka berbelanja di pasar daripada berbelanja di pusat perbelanjaan. Dia bilang kemarin, 'Barang-barang di pasar yang paling murah!' Istri saya berbelanja di pasar setiap hari Jum'at. Rumah kami kecil, tetapi di rumah kami ada pelajar asing tahun ini. Dia orang Australia dan namanya Ian Webb. Dia akan pulang pada bulan Nopember.

a Where does Bima work?
b What is his wife's occupation?
c Why does she prefer shopping at the market?
d When does she go to the market?
e Is their house large or small?
f Who is Ian?
g When is Ian returning to Australia?

12 Wati receives a text message from Linda, who is first to arrive at their hotel room. List the room's features.

> Wati, di kamar hotel ada fasilitas internet dan AC. Ada kamar mandi di dalam. Ada air panas dan pancuran mandi.

13 Tono receives a text message from Tini not long after he leaves her in a queue at the till. Translate her message.

> Tono, di kasir tidak ada kembalian. Saya tidak ada uang pas. Kamu ada uang lima puluh ribu rupiah?

14 Read the notes about Ningsih and use the information to help her fill in the hotel's registration form.

Nama dia Ningsih. Nama keluarganya Suparman. Ningsih bekerja di sebuah LSM. Dia lahir pada tanggal dua belas Juli tahun seribu sembilan ratus delapan puluh. Dia tinggal di Jalan Sadikin nomor tiga puluh empat. Rumahnya di kota Jakarta. Kode posnya satu-nol-satu-enam-dua-dua. Nomor telpon dia kosong-dua-satu-lima-tiga-enam-lima-tujuh-kosong-satu.

Hotel Papandayan

a Nama Tamu: _____
b Tanggal Lahir: _____
c Pekerjaan: _____
d Alamat: _____
e Kota: _____
f Kode Pos: _____
g No. Telepon: _____

15 Linda and Saul Curtis are making enquiries into renting a house in Bali. Read Linda's email to a local property agent and answer the following questions.

YTH Bapak/Ibu,

Apa kabar? Nama saya Linda Curtis. Saya dan suami saya Saul sudah tinggal di Indonesia selama satu tahun. Tahun ini kami mau menyewa rumah di Bali untuk tiga bulan, dari bulan Juni sampai bulan Agustus. Kami perlu tiga kamar tidur dan dua kamar mandi. Kami kurang suka dapur yang kecil. Kami akan senang kalau ada teras yang besar dan kolam renang juga. Kami bisa bayar uang sewa dalam dolar atau rupiah. Tolong hubungi kami di 0811-2873-62590. Saya tunggu kabar dari Anda.

Salam,

Linda

a How long do they want to rent the house for?
b How many bedrooms and bathrooms do they need?
c What would they not like?
d What extras would they enjoy?
e What did Linda write about the rent money?

7 Selamat jalan!

Have a good journey!

In this unit you will learn how to:
- ▶ *talk about different modes of transport.*
- ▶ *order and buy tickets.*
- ▶ *ask for and give the time.*
- ▶ *talk about the locations here, there, and over there.*

CEFR: *Can indicate time.;* **(A1)** *Can get simple information about travel, use of public transport, and buy tickets.* **(A2)**

Transportation

Crossing the Indonesian archipelago by **kapal terbang** or **pesawat terbang** (*aeroplane*) gives you spectacular views of the country's volcanoes. Overland transport such as the intercity **bus** (*bus*) and the **kereta api** (*train*), however, allows you to **naik** (*get on*) or **turun** (*get off*) in smaller towns and cities. Although there is no **kereta bawah tanah** (*underground train*) in Indonesia, local travel can be done by bus, **taksi** (*taxi*), or the **ojek** (*motorcycle service*) that takes you anywhere you want to go if you are comfortable riding as a **penumpang** (*passenger*) on a motorcycle. Remember to ask how much the **ongkos** (*cost, charge*) is before the **perjalanan** (*journey*) begins. Using **kendaraan umum** (*public transport*) can be convenient, but metered rides are offered only by taxi companies. If you wish to hire a **mobil** (*car*), you may drive it yourself if you have a valid license. In tourist areas, hiring a **sepeda motor** (*motorcycle*) or **sepeda** (*bicycle*) is a great way to get around. To get to Indonesia's smaller islands, cross the waters by **kapal** (*ship*) or **feri** (*ferry*). Transport routes are busiest during **Lebaran,** the holiday marking the end of the fasting month, when many celebrants travel to visit their families.

 What do you think the phrase for *trip fare* might be?

Vocabulary builder

 07.01 **Look at the words and phrases and complete the English translations. Then listen to the recording and imitate the pronunciation of the speakers.**

TRAVELLING

berangkat	*depart*
sampai	*arrive*
ganti	*switch* (v.), *change* (v.)
kembali	*return* (v.)
loket	*(ticket) window, counter*
karcis	*ticket*
jurusan	*destination, heading (for)*
tiket pulang pergi	_____ *ticket*
tiket sekali jalan	_____ *ticket*
bagasi	*luggage*
koper	*suitcase*
selamat jalan	*have a good journey*
selamat tinggal	*goodbye* (to people you leave behind)

LOCATION

sini	*here*
situ	*there*
sana	*over there*

TIME

jam	*hour*
menit	_____
kurang	*less, minus*
lewat	*past*
seperempat	*a quarter*
setengah	*half*

The word **pukul** is also used to mean *hour*. This use is highly formal, usually reserved for the news and telling the time on the radio and television.

NEW EXPRESSIONS

buatkan	*create (for)*
tentu	*of course*
baru	*recently, just, newly*

datang	come, arrive
terlambat	slow, late

Conversation 1

 07.02 *Jon is at the airport having missed his flight and needing another.*

1 What form of identification does Jon provide?

Soraya	Bisa saya bantu, Pak?
Jon	Masih ada pesawat terbang ke Bali hari ini?
Soraya	Ada, Pak. Ada pesawat yang berangkat pada jam empat kurang seperempat sore.
Jon	Baiklah. Saya mau membeli satu tiket.
Soraya	Bapak mau naik kelas ekonomi atau bisnis?
Jon	Saya mau naik kelas ekonomi.
Soraya	Pulang pergi atau sekali jalan, Pak?
Jon	Pulang pergi.
Soraya	Kapan Bapak mau kembali ke Jakarta?
Jon	Saya belum tahu. Anda bisa buatkan saya tiket tanggal terbuka?
Soraya	Ya. Bisa. Saya boleh lihat paspornya, Pak?
Jon	Tentu boleh. Ini paspor saya.
Soraya	Ada bagasi, Pak?
Jon	Ya, ada satu koper.
Soraya	Ini tiketnya. Selamat jalan, Pak.
Jon	Selamat tinggal.

tiket tanggal	open-date
terbuka	*ticket*

2 Find the expressions in the conversation that mean:
   a travel in economy class   _____
   b I don't know yet.   _____
   c Goodbye.   _____

3 Read or listen again and answer the questions.
   a When is the flight departing?
   b What kind of ticket does Jon buy?
   c What luggage does Jon have?

07.03 Now listen to the lines from the conversation and repeat. Be sure to pay attention to the pronunciation.

# Language discovery

1. **Look at the sentences from the conversation. Put the words in English into Indonesian.**
   a Dia mau (*travel in economy class*).
   b Pesawat itu berangkat (*at a quarter to four in the afternoon*).

1 TRAVELLING

When discussing travel, the word **naik** (*get on*) can be used to mean *travelling in/on, going by, taking, riding*. You can also use **naik** to mean *by*. For example, **kembali ke kantor naik bus** means *return to the office by bus*.

Setiap hari dia naik kendaraan umum ke kantor.

Every day he takes public transport to the office.

Saya pergi naik bus dan dia naik sepeda motornya ke Palu.

I am going by bus and she is riding her motorcycle to Palu.

2 THE TIME

When telling the time, start with the hour. For example, **jam tiga** (*three o'clock*). If it is *five minutes past the hour*, add **lewat lima menit**. If it is *five minutes to the hour*, add **kurang lima menit**. Then, mention the time of day as necessary.

Sekarang jam tiga lewat lima menit sore.

It is now five minutes past three o'clock in the afternoon.

> You can leave out the word **menit** (*minute*) once you are comfortable without it.

The word **setengah** is also used in telling the time, but it is the reverse of the British usage of *half* so that **setengah dua** (*half two*) means *half past one*.

Saya sampai pada jam setengah dua siang.

I arrive at half past one in the afternoon.

Indonesians also use **seperempat** (*a quarter*) in place of **lima belas menit** (*fifteen minutes*).

Kakek berangkat pada jam enam kurang seperempat pagi.

Grandfather left at a quarter to six in the morning.

To ask about the time, use **jam berapa** (*what hour*).

Jam berapa sekarang? Jam empat.

What time is it now? Four o'clock.

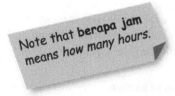

Note that berapa jam means how many hours.

Practice

1 Put the following sentences into English.

   a Jon naik kapal terbang ke Bali.

   b Ita naik sepeda ke rumah ibunya.

   c Dimas naik mobil ke kantor.

2 Put the following times into Indonesian.

   a 12:15pm

   b 09:50am

   c 07:30pm

 3 07.04 **Now use the times to prepare responses to the questions below. Then, listen and answer in real time. Do this as many times as you need to for it to become second nature.**

Jam berapa kereta api berangkat?

Pada jam berapa ferinya akan sampai di Lombok?

Untuk jam berapa Anda mau memesan taksi?

Pronunciation

There are two pronunciations of the letter **e** in Indonesian. They can both be found in the word **sepeda** (*bicycle*). In older reading material, the second **e** may be spelled as **é** to differentiate the sounds. Currently, the only way to familiarize yourself with the different pronunciations is to hear the words being spoken.

 07.05 **Listen to the two pronunciations of the letter e and repeat.**

1 sepeda
2 mereka
3 sewa
4 seperempat
5 kereta

 Speaking

1 07.06 **Look at Helen's schedule and talk about it in Indonesian using the 12-hour clock.**

07:00	go to the office by car
12:00	go to lunch by bus
13:30	return to the office by motorcycle service
17:20	return home by car

2 **Now talk about your own schedule in Indonesian.**

Conversation 2

 07.07 *Linda has just got off the bus at a station. She now needs to get on a different bus to get to Solo.*

1 How much time is left before the bus departs?

Linda	Permisi, Pak. Saya harus ganti bus. Di mana saya bisa naik bus jurusan Solo?
Abdul	Bus itu baru berangkat. Mau ke mana, Bu?
Linda	Mau ke Solo.
Abdul	Bus berikutnya bus jurusan Semarang. Bus itu berhenti di Solo. Naik bus itu dan turun di Solo.
Linda	Di mana saya bisa naik bus jurusan Semarang?
Abdul	Ibu bisa naik bus jurusan Semarang di sini.
Linda	Jam berapa busnya berangkat?
Abdul	Busnya berangkat pada jam satu lewat seperempat siang.
Linda	Jam berapa sekarang?
Abdul	Jam satu kurang sepuluh.
Linda	Oh, masih ada dua puluh lima menit.
Abdul	Ya, Ibu ada waktu. Ibu tidak akan terlambat.
Linda	Di mana saya bisa membeli karcis bus?
Abdul	Di dalam bus atau di loket, tetapi lebih baik di loket. Loketnya di situ.

berhenti	*stop* (v.)
berikut	*following, next*
waktu	*time*

2 Match the Indonesian to the English.

a Mau ke Solo.
b Jam berapa sekarang?
c Jam berapa busnya berangkat?

1 *What time is it now?*
2 *What time is the bus leaving?*
3 *I'm going to Solo.*

3 Check, then cover up your answers and see if you can say them without looking at the conversation.

4 Read or listen again and answer the following questions.

a What bus does Linda need to get?
b When is the next bus departing?
c Where can Linda buy a bus ticket?

5 07.08 Now listen to the lines from the conversation and repeat. Then listen to Linda's lines and respond as Abdul.

 Language discovery

1 Look at the sentences from the conversation. Find the sentences in Indonesian that mean the following.

    a You can get on the bus heading for Semarang here. The ticket booth is there.

    b That bus just departed.

    c Where are you going, Madam?

1 *HERE, THERE,* AND *OVER THERE*

When you use the location words **sini** (*here*), **situ** (*there*), and **sana** (*over there*), they should always be combined with either the preposition **di** (*at/in/on*), **ke** (*to*), or **dari** (*from*).

naik bus di sini	*get on the bus here*
loket di situ	*the ticket booth is there*
terbang ke sana dari sini	*fly over there from here*

2 IF SOMETHING JUST HAPPENED

The word **baru** (*new*) can be used to talk about how something only recently or just happened. For example, you can say that **dia baru datang** to mean *he recently came* or *he just came*.

3 WHEN 'WANT (TO GO)' MEANS 'GOING'

The phrase **mau pergi** (*want to go*) can also mean *intend to go* or *are going* if it is used when you're already on your way. Whilst you're travelling, you may be asked, **Kamu mau pergi ke mana?** to mean *Where are you going?* Since this question is often asked in everyday situations when people are in a hurry, the pronoun **Anda** or **kamu** (*you*) and the word **pergi** (*go*) is often omitted so that the question becomes **Mau ke mana?** (*Going where?*) You can reply, **Mau ke Solo**, for example, to mean *I'm going to Solo.*

 Practice

1 Put the following sentences into Indonesian.
   a Bus Anda akan berhenti di situ.
   b Berapa ongkos perjalanan dari sini ke sana?

2 Put the following sentences into English.
   a Pesawat terbang dari Ambon baru sampai.
   b Dia baru beli tiket.

 3 07.09 Practise asking and answering questions about where you want to go or are going to go.

 Listening

1 07.10 Listen to the dialogue and answer the following questions.

Berapa lama	How long, What is the duration of
kira-kira	roughly, at a guess
jalan kaki	walk, travel on foot
sewaktu	while, when

   a What times are the trains?
   b How long is the journey?
   c How much is the ticket that she buys?

2 07.11 Listen to the dialogue and match the travel plan to the suggested transport option.

a travelling to Trawas	**1** *by taxi*
b going to Madura	**2** *by motorcycle service*
c going into the city	**3** *go on foot*
d getting to the market	**4** *by ship*
e when you have no time	**5** *by car*

3 07.12 **Read the questions below and prepare responses that are true for you. Then, listen and respond in real time.**

> Jam berapa sekarang?

> Pada jam berapa Anda berangkat dari rumah?

> Pada jam berapa Anda sampai di kantor?

Reading and writing

1 **Samuel Lim has written a letter to his Indonesian grandmother about his travels in Indonesia so far.**

> YTH Nenek,
>
> Aku datang ke Indonesia pada bulan September. Pada bulan Oktober, aku naik kereta api dari Jakarta ke Yogyakarta. Tiketnya tidak mahal. Perjalanan dari sini ke sana sembilan jam. Kalau naik pesawat dari Jakarta ke Yogyakarta hanya satu jam. Sewaktu di Yogyakarta aku suka naik ojek dan jalan kaki. Aku kembali ke Jakarta naik bus. Di Jakarta, aku naik taksi.
>
> Samuel

2 **Imagine you're travelling in Indonesia. Write a letter about your travels and how you're getting around.**

Go further

In Indonesia, there are three recognised time zones, which you might come across in the news or whilst travelling eastwards or westwards from one end of the country to the other.

Waktu Indonesia Barat (WIB)   Western Indonesia Time

Waktu Indonesia Tengah (WITA) Central Indonesia Time

Waktu Indonesia Timur (WIT)   Eastern Indonesia Time

On the news broadcast from the capital Jakarta, for example, you would hear the time announced as **pukul sembilan malam WIB** (*nine o'clock in the evening Western Indonesia Time*).

If you want to talk about getting around at certain times of day instead of at a specific hour, you can combine the concepts you have learned so far.

1 **Complete the English translations.**

   a pada pagi hari   *In the* _____

   b pada siang hari   *In the day*

   c pada sore hari   *In the* _____

   d pada malam hari   *In the* _____ *or at night*

2 **Put the following sentences into Indonesian.**

   a I arrived in Indonesia at night.

   b I departed in the morning.

   c I will take the underground train in the early afternoon.

   d She will come to Lembang by train in the late afternoon.

As you have seen, the word **datang** can mean both *come* and *arrive*. When there is a difference, it lies in the preposition you use so that **datang di** means *arrive at* and **datang ke** means *come to*. The combination **datang dari** can mean both *arrive from* and *come from*, whether the place refers to your last place of embarkation or where your journey began.

 3 07.13 **Read the questions below and prepare your own responses. Then, listen and respond. Do this as many times as you need to for it to become second nature.**

   a Pukul berapa sekarang di kota Anda?

   b Anda datang dari mana?

   c Kamu mau datang ke rumahku?

   d Selamat datang di Indonesia! Kapan kamu sampai?

Test yourself

1 Put the words in English into Indonesian.

Amir naik (*aeroplane*) **dari Jakarta ke Medan dengan** (*one-way ticket*)**.** (*Journey*) **dia kira-kira dua jam. Di Medan Amir** (*went by car*) **ke rumah orang tuanya. Amir dan Samsul, adik laki-laki Amir,** (*travelled by taxi*) **ke bank mereka. Malam itu, Amir** (*rode a motorcycle*) **ke Belawan. Dari Belawan, dia** (*got on*) **feri** (*heading for*) **Kepulauan Riau dan** (*got off*) **di Pulau Batam.**

2 Put the following sentences into English.

  a .jam empat kurang dua puluh sore
  b jam tujuh lewat seperempat pagi
  c jam setengah sembilan malam
  d jam dua belas siang

3 Unscramble the words to make full sentences.

  a jurusan datang Pada Madiun berapa jam kereta ?
  a malam mereka sebelas pada Mobil jam sampai.
  a mau Jam berangkat Anda berapa ?
  a berapa berangkat pesawat Jam berikutnya ?

4 Choose the correct word to match the phrases with the English translations.

  a datang ke *sini / sana*   *come here*
  b sampai di *sini / situ*   *arrive there*
  c berangkat dari *sini / sana*   *depart from over there*

5 Put the following sentences into Indonesian.

  a I just returned from Gili.
  b The passengers just got off the plane.

6 Choose the one that doesn't mean '*Where are you going?*'

  a Mau ke mana?   **c** Anda mau pergi ke mana?
  b Mau di mana?

SELF CHECK	
I CAN ...	
○	talk about different modes of transport.
○	order and buy tickets.
○	ask for and give the time.
○	talk about the locations *here*, *there*, and *over there*.

8

Mari memesan! Kamu mau makan apa?

Let's order! What do you want to eat?

In this unit you will learn how to:
▶ *talk about food.*
▶ *read and order items from a menu.*
▶ *ask for and understand suggestions.*
▶ *ask for the bill.*
▶ *talk about doing things together.*

CEFR (A2): *Can understand short, simple texts such as menus. Can make and respond to suggestions.*

 Cuisine

Most Indonesians prefer savoury breakfast dishes, but eating **roti** (*bread*) is now more common and **roti bakar** (*toast, grilled sandwich*) is served in hotels and as **enak** (*delicious*) street food. Lunch may come in the form of **sepiring nasi goreng** (*a plate of fried rice*) or **semangkok mie telur rebus** (*a bowl of egg noodle soup*), single-dish meals served to those on the go. In the afternoon, you may be interested in tasting **secangkir kopi luwak** (*a cup of civet coffee*) with some **kue bolu kukus** (*steamed sponge cake*) or enjoying **segelas jus alpukat** (*a glass of avocado juice*), often mixed with chocolate and served cold. When dining together, Indonesians enjoy sharing dishes served all at the same time instead of in succession. A luxurious but harmonious meal would contain a combination of **ikan** (*fish*), meat such as **daging ayam** (*chicken*), shellfish such as **udang** (*shrimp*), **sayur-sayur** (*vegetables*), **tahu** (*tofu*), and **tempe** (*fermented soy bean patty*) cooked in a variety of ways. Many Indonesian dishes are prepared using **santan** (*coconut milk*) or soy sauce, but each regional **masakan** (*cuisine*) is typified by a particular flavour or ingredient. Javanese cooking, for example, is **manis** (*sweet*), Madurese food is **asin** (*salty*), and Padang cuisine is **pedas** (*spicy*).

 If **dua porsi nasi** means *two portions of rice*, how would you say *a portion of rice*?

Vocabulary builder

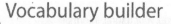

08.01 **Look at the words and phrases. First, match the Indonesian to the English. Next, use the words in the box to complete the English translations. Then, listen to the recording and imitate the pronunciation of the speakers.**

COOKING METHODS

a **goreng**
b **rebus**
c **bakar/panggang**
d **kukus**
e **tumis**

1 *to boil, boiled*
2 *to roast/grill, roasted/grilled*
3 *to stir-fry, stir-fried*
4 *to fry, fried*
5 *to steam, steamed*

> While some Indonesian dishes have individual names, many are also listed in menus according to how they are prepared.

POPULAR MENU ITEMS

soup, prawn cracker, curry, meat skewer

krupuk udang	_____
sate	_____
kare	_____
sop	_____

OTHER STAPLE FOODS

singkong	*cassava*	**sagu**	*sago*
bubur	*porridge*	**lontong**	*steamed rice cake*

NEW EXPRESSIONS

kalian	*you, your (plural, informal)*
ingin	*want, wish*
pesan	*order (v.)*
minum	*drink (v.)*
minta	*request, ask for*
semua	*all*
yang	*the one/ones that is/are, the ... one/ ones*
ambilkan	*to fetch*
selesai	*to be finished, to be done*
bon	*cheque, bill*
angkat	*to lift (up), clear (coll., v.)*
bersama	*together, (along) with*
bagaimana kalau	*how would it be if, (coll.) what about*

DRINKS

air	*water*
kopi	*coffee*
teh	*tea*
es teh	*iced tea*
air jeruk	*a mix of orange juice, sugar, and water*
jus jeruk	*orange juice*
susu kedelai	*soy milk*
bir	*beer*

To avoid drinking unsanitary water, ask for **air mineral** (mineral water) or **air botol** (bottled water).

USEFUL WORDS

panas	*hot*	**dingin**	*cold*
hangat	*warm*	**tawar**	*plain*
pahit	*bitter*	**asam**	*sour*
garam	*salt*	**lada**	*pepper*

If the high level of sweetness in Indonesian drinks does not suit your tastes, you can order your drink **tawar** (*plain*), for example as **teh tawar** (*unsweetened tea*), before adding your preferred amount of **gula** (*sugar*). The exception is unsweetened coffee, which must be ordered as **kopi pahit** (*bitter coffee*).

sapi	*cow*
kambing	*goat*
babi	*pig*
kepiting	*crab*
jeruk	*orange*
pisang	*banana*
kelapa	*coconut*
kacang	*nut, pea, bean*
jagung	*corn*
kentang	*potato*

When talking about food, the words for land animals must be prefaced with the word for meat. For example, **babi** is *pig* but **daging babi** is *pork*.

08.02 **Listen to the drinks, useful words, and shopping list and imitate the pronunciation of the speakers.**

 **Conversation 1**

08.03 *A family of three arrives at a restaurant.*

1 What drinks do they order?

Pelayan	Selamat datang di Restoran Ibu Munir.
Ibu	Selamat siang. Ada meja untuk empat orang?
Pelayan	Ada. Silakan duduk. Ini menunya.
Ibu	Anak-anak, kalian ingin makan apa?
Tono	Saya ingin makan kare ikan dan tempe goreng. Saya ingin minum es teh manis.
Tini	Pak, apakah saya boleh meminta secangkir teh panas dan sepiring mie goreng sayur?
Pelayan	Tentu boleh. Ibu mau memesan apa?
Ibu	Saya ingin mencoba mienya. Yang mana enak?
Pelayan	Semua mie kami enak.
Ibu	Saya suka yang pedas. Yang mana pedas?
Pelayan	Mie telur kami pedas. Ibu ingin coba mie telur?
Ibu	Baiklah. Saya ingin pesan semangkok mie telur rebus, segelas es kopi, dan dua porsi sate ayam.
Tono	Kami juga mau sop bayam, air dingin tanpa es, dan nasi untuk dua orang.

[The waiter leaves and returns with their order.]

Pelayan	Ini pesanan Anda. Ini minuman-minuman Anda. Dan ini makanan Anda datang sekarang.
Tono	Pak, tolong ambilkan saya satu sedotan.
Pelayan	Maaf. Ini sedotannya. Selamat makan.

duduk	*sit*
meja	*table*
bayam	*spinach*
sedotan	*straw*

2 Find the expressions in the conversation that mean:

  a Which one is the delicious one? _____
  b And here is your food coming now. _____
  c Please fetch me a straw. _____

3 Read or listen again and answer the questions.

  a What has the mother ordered?
  b What was Tono missing?
  c What do you think *Selamat makan* means?

4 08.04 **Now listen to the lines from the conversation and repeat. Be sure to pay attention to the pronunciation.**

 Language discovery

1 Look at the sentences from the conversation. Put the words in English into Indonesian.

- **a** Ibu mau (*order*) apa?
- **b** Ini (*order*) Anda.
- **c** Saya ingin memesan (*a cup*) teh panas.
- **d** Saya suka (*the spicy ones*). Yang mana (*spicy*)?

1 MORE ABOUT VERBS

One important verbal prefix is **meX-**, the **X** standing for a letter that changes depending on the first letter of the verb's root word. For example, the word **pesan** becomes **memesan** (*order*).

If the root word begins with a vowel, **meX-** becomes **meng-** so that **ajar** becomes **mengajar** (*teach*).

If the root word begins with b, f, or p, **meX-** becomes **mem-** so that **beli** becomes **membeli** (*buy*) and, because you have to drop the p, **pakai** becomes **memakai** (*wear, use*).

If the root word begins with c, d, j, t, sy, or z, **meX-** becomes **men-** so that **cari** becomes **mencari** (*look for*), **jual** becomes **menjual** (*sell*). You would also drop the t so that, for example, **tunggu** becomes **menunggu** (*wait*).

If the root word for the verb begins with g, h, k, or kh, **meX-** becomes **meng-** so that **ganti** becomes **mengganti** (*change*).

If the root word begins with s, **meX-** becomes **meny-** so that the word **sewa** becomes **menyewa** (*rent*).

If the root word begins with l, m, n, ny, ng, r, w, or y, there is no change and **meX-** becomes **me-** so that **masak**, for example, becomes **memasak** (*cook*).

Whenever you come across an unfamiliar verb that begins with **meX-**, knowing how **X** changes helps you look up the verb's meaning because in a dictionary, a verb is always listed under its root word.

Native speakers sometimes drop the **me-** whilst keeping the related **X** sound change. For example, when **goreng** is transformed into **menggoreng** (*fry*), what you might hear in everyday speech is **nggoreng**.

2 TURNING VERBS INTO NOUNS USING THE SUFFIX –AN

A basic Indonesian noun can be created out of a basic verb by adding the suffix **–an** to the end of the original word. Adding **–an** to **pesan** (*to order*) will give you **pesanan** (*an order, what you order*), for example. Adding **–an** to **masak** (*cook*) will give you **masakan** (*cooking* or *cuisine, what you cook or dish*).

3 USING THE SE– PREFIX WHEN ORDERING

As you have previously seen, the **se–** prefix is used in counting to mean *one* of something. When ordering food or drink, attach the **se–** prefix to the tableware or container used for serving.

Saya mau semangkok (or satu mangkok) bubur ayam.

I want one bowl of chicken porridge.

Saya mau sebotol (or satu botol) bir.

I want one bottle of beer.

When you order an item without specifying how you want it served, you should use **satu** (*one*) instead of the **se–** prefix.

Saya mau memesan satu es teh tawar.

I want to order one unsweetened (or plain) iced tea.

4 SUGGESTIONS

While you can ask for a suggestion by asking **Apa saran Anda?** (*What is your suggestion?*), Indonesians are more likely to first state their preferences before asking for suitable menu items to be pointed out to them. For example, you first state that you like **yang asin** (*the salty ones* or *the ones that are salty*) to mean you like **makanan yang asin** (*food that is salty*). Then, you would ask **Yang mana asin?** (*Which ones are salty?*)

Saya suka yang tidak pedas. Yang mana tidak pedas?

I like the ones that are not spicy. Which ones are not spicy?

Saya mau minuman yang manis. Yang mana manis?

I want a drink that is sweet. Which ones are sweet?

Food or drink suggestions are usually made by asking people to **coba** (*try*) something or whether they wish to try something.

Kalau Anda suka yang manis, cobalah jus jeruk.

If you like the ones that are sweet, try the orange juice.

Anda ingin coba krupuk udang?

Do you wish to try the prawn crackers?

 Practice

1 **Give the Indonesian root words for the following verbs, then complete the English translation of the verbs.**
   a merebus   _____   _____
   b menggoreng   _____   _____
   c mengukus   _____   _____

2 **Turn the verbs into nouns and complete the English translation of the nouns.**
   a makan   _____   _____
   b minum   _____   _____
   c masak   _____   _____

3 **Put the following sentences into English.**
   a Kakek ingin memesan secangkir kopi luwak.
   b Adik perempuanku tidak mau semangkok sup ayam.
   c Mereka ingin seporsi ikan bakar kecap.

 4 08.05 **Practise telling others what you like and then asking for suitable suggestions.**

> Saya suka yang tidak pahit. Yang mana tidak pahit?

Pronunciation

 08.06 **Several Indonesian words have two or more accepted pronunciations either because they can be spelled in different ways or due to regional differences. Listen to how the following words are pronounced and repeat.**

1 telur   telor

2 santan   santen

3 asam   asem

4 sop   sup

5 saos   saus

 # Speaking

08.07 **Read the questions below and prepare your own responses. Then, listen and respond in real time. Do this as many times as you need to for it to become second nature.**

Anda ingin memesan apa?

Anda mau meja untuk berapa orang?

 # Conversation 2

08.08 *Ani and Affandi are at the end of their meal.*

1 What does Affandi think is very delicious?

Ani	Makanan di rumah makan ini enak, ya? Kamu mau satu porsi ikan panggang lagi?
Affandi	Rasanya enak sekali tetapi aku sudah kenyang. Kamu masih lapar?
Ani	Tidak. Kita sudah selesai, ya?
Affandi	Ya. Sudah. Aku akan minta bonnya. Permisi, Pak. Kami boleh minta bonnya?
Ani	Dia tidak dengar kamu. Coba minta sekali lagi.

Affandi	Permisi, Pak. Tolong ambilkan bonnya.
Pelayan	Ya, Pak. Saya ambilkan. Sudah selesai makan, ya? Kami boleh angkat semua dari meja?
Affandi	Ya. Silakan. Terima kasih. Ani, kamu mau makan bersama lagi pada hari Jum'at?
Ani	Maaf. Jum'at ini saya akan makan bersama Yati.
Affandi	Kalau begitu, bagaimana kalau hari Sabtu?
Ani	Sabtu? Bisa. Aku bisa makan bersama kamu pada hari Sabtu.

rasa	flavour, taste, feel
lapar	hungry
kenyang	full
dengar	hear

2 Find the expressions in the conversation that mean:
   a very delicious   _____
   b still hungry   _____
   c have finished   _____
   d eat together   _____

3 Check, then cover up your answers and see if you can say them without looking at the conversation.

4 Read or listen again and answer the following questions.
   a What do you think *rumah makan* means?
   b Why does Affandi have to flag the waiter twice?
   c What does the waiter ask for permission to do?
   d d When are they planning to eat together again?

5 08.09 **Now listen to the lines from the conversation and repeat. Then listen to Affandi's lines and respond as Ani.**

Language discovery

1 Look at the sentences from the conversation. Put the words in English into Indonesian..
   a Kamu mau (*another plate of curry*)?
   b Tolong (*fetch the cheque*).
   c Kamu mau makan (*together*) pada akhir minggu?

1 ORDERING MORE

You can use the word **lagi** (*again, more*) to order more food or drink by placing it after the thing or things you want more of.

Satu gelas air jeruk hangat lagi, ya?

Another (or one more) glass of warm orangeade, please.

2 ASKING FOR THE CHEQUE

Traditionally, the cheque is calculated by the cashier and not the servers. Hence, you could ask the waiter to fetch the cheque or make a request for the cheque. Where a cheque is not available, for instance at a street stall, you can ask **Berapa semua?** (*How much is it all?*)

Tolong ambilkan bonnya.	*Please fetch the cheque.*
Saya boleh minta bonnya?	*May I ask for the cheque?*

3 DOING THINGS TOGETHER

The word **bersama** (*together*) can be used after verbs when you want to say that you are doing an activity with others.

Tjin dan Sri makan bersama. Saya makan bersama Santi.

Tjin and Sri eat together. I eat (along) with Santi.

Anda mau makan siang bersama kami?

Do you want to eat lunch with us?

You can also invite others to do an activity with you or signal the start of a shared activity using the word **Mari** (*Let's, Come*).

Mari makan.   *Let's eat. Come eat.*

 Practice

1 **Put the following sentences into English.**
   a Ayah mau sepiring nasi ayam lagi.
   b Tiga porsi sate kambing lagi, ya?

2 **Put the following sentences into Indonesian.**
   a Please fetch our cheque.
   b Please ask for the cheque.

3 08.10 **Practise inviting others to eat with you.**

 Listening

dibawa pulang	*carried/taken away (lit. taken home)*
dibungkus	*wrapped (to go)*
sehat	*healthy*
haus	*thirsty*

1 08.11 **Linda is at a food stall, ordering lunch. Listen to the dialogue and answer the following questions.**

  a Is the food to be eaten there or to be taken away?
  b What does the vendor say is healthy and delicious?
  c What does Linda take to go?

> Vendors who sell drinks in glass bottles will need those bottles back. Ask for your drink to be **dibungkus** (*wrapped*) and they will pour it into a container for you.

2 08.12 **Read the menu and prepare a takeaway order that you'd like to eat. Then, listen and respond in real time.**

Mau pesan apa?

Menu Warung Pak Bejo

sate sapi	pisang goreng
udang bakar	tumis bayam
ayam lada hitam	kentang goreng
sate Padang	nasi
sop tahu	mie
kepiting asam manis	lontong

Reading and writing

1 **Shinta and Amir have left a meal on the dining table for their children to eat. Read their e-mail to the children.**

Anak-anak, Ibu dan Ayah akan makan malam di rumah kolega kami malam ini. Kalian harus makan bersama, ya? Di meja makan ada makanan yang sehat untuk kalian semua. Ada nasi, ayam panggang, tumis kacang panjang, dan singkong rebus. Ada juga kue bolu kukus coklat dari Nenek. Selamat makan!

2 **You have prepared some delicious Indonesian dishes and drinks for your friends but unfortunately you can't be there to enjoy the lunch with them. Complete the note.**

Teman-teman, maaf, ya? Saya tidak bisa ...

Go further

The basic Indonesian cutlery combination is the **garpu** (*fork*) and the **sendok** (*spoon*), but eating with one's hands is a valued tradition. It would be polite to wash or clean your hands before eating and to use your right hand to convey food to your mouth.

1 **Match the Indonesian to the English.**

a	sumpit	*knife*
b	sendok teh	*kitchen knife*
c	pisau	*chopsticks*
d	pisau dapur	*cutlery*
e	sendok garpu	*teaspoon*

CONDIMENTS

2 Use the words in the box to complete the English translations.

> sweet soy sauce,   chilli sauce,
> soy sauce

a kecap asin   _____
b kecap manis   _____
c saos sambal   _____

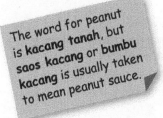

The word for peanut is **kacang tanah**, but **saos kacang** or **bumbu kacang** is usually taken to mean peanut sauce.

If you have food allergies, you can easily tell others that you **tidak boleh** (*may not*) eat or drink something. You can also explain that you have an allergy using the prefix **ber-** (*to have*) or the word **punya** (*to have*) with the word **alergi** (*allergy*).

Saya tidak boleh makan dan minum yang manis.
I am not allowed to eat and drink sweet things.

Saya beralergi (or punya alergi) kacang tanah.
I have an allergy to peanuts.

---

3 08.13 Read the questions below and prepare your own responses. Then, listen and respond. Check the glossary if there are words you don't know.

a Anda perlu sendok garpu?
b Anda boleh minum minuman beralkohol?
c Anda punya alergi?

Test yourself

1 Put the following sentences into English.
    a Kami akan menunggu makanan kami.
    b Pak Bejo membungkus minuman mereka.
    c Saya membawa pulang masakan Leslie.

2 Insert the **–an** suffix into the sentences to correct them.
    a Bubur sagu makan dari Maluku.
    b Babi panggang masak tradisional di Toba.
    c Kopi luwak minum mahal.

3 Put the following sentences into Indonesian.
    a I wish to order a glass of cold water and two glasses of beer.
    b His wife wants to eat a portion of steamed rice cake.
    c My children want one grilled fish and two fried noodles.

4 Unscramble the words to make full sentences.
    a tidak mana Yang asin?
    b manis, Anda goreng suka singkong yang cobalah Kalau .
    c coba kedelai ingin kami susu Anda?

5 Use the words in the box to recreate the phrases below.

> satu, lagi,   nasi, teh,
> dua,   lagi,   porsi,

    a another tea
    b two more portions of rice

6 Match the Indonesian to the English.
    a Berapa semua?   **1** Please fetch the cheque.
    b Tolong ambilkan bonnya.   **2** May I ask for the cheque?
    c Saya boleh minta bonnya?   **3** How much is it all?

7 Put the words in English into Indonesian.
    a Mereka mau memasak (*together*).
    b Bernard mau makan (*with*) saya?
    c (*Let's*) makan.

SELF CHECK

I CAN ...

- ⭘ talk about food
- ⭘ read and order items from a menu
- ⭘ ask for and understand suggestions
- ⭘ ask for the bill
- ⭘ talk about doing things together

9 Bagaimana cara jalan kaki ke bioskop?

How do I walk to the cinema?

In this unit you will learn how to:
▶ *ask for and understand directions.*
▶ *understand sequences using words and numbers.*
▶ *accept or refuse an offer of help.*
▶ *recognise warnings.*
▶ *ask and explain how to do something.*

CEFR: *Can recognize familiar words concerning concrete surroundings.* **(A1)**; *Can understand everyday signs.* **(A2)**

Finding your way

One of the **tempat-tempat** (*places*) worth visiting when you visit a historic city in Indonesia is the **alun-alun kota** (*town square*), where people gather for events or simply pass the time. Take public transport if it is **jauh** (*far*) from where you are and try walking if it is **dekat** (*near*). If you are worried about losing your way, know that Indonesians are always happy to assist people who are **tersesat** (*lost)* or in need of **bantuan** (*help*). Some may even offer to **antar** (*escort*) you to your destination or ask you to **ikut** (*follow*) them there. Their generosity can be a great help because every culture has its own **cara** (*method*) of navigating and it may take practice to make sense of the directions you get. Asking about what you'll find along the way is also helpful, not to mention a fantastic way of making your own local **peta** (*map*). First-time visitors to the country may find the lack of a **trotoar** (*pavement*) along many streets disconcerting at first so do go **hati-hati** (*carefully*) when **berjalan-jalan** (*walking about*) and **menyeberang** (*crossing*) roads. Go **pelan-pelan** (*slowly*) instead of **cepat-cepat** (*quickly*) and enjoy what the city has to offer.

How would you say *I need help* in Indonesian?

Vocabulary builder

 09.01 **Look at the words and phrases and match the Indonesian places to the English. Then listen to the recording and imitate the pronunciation of the speakers.**

PLACES

a	kantor pos	1	*crossing, crosswalk*
b	kantor polisi	2	*cinema*
c	stasiun kereta	3	*embassy*
d	halte bus	4	*public toilet*
e	bandara, bandar udara	5	*post office*
f	kedutaan	6	*police station*
g	warnet	7	*train station*
h	bioskop	8	*parking space, car park*
i	tempat parkir	9	*airport*
j	tempat penyeberangan	10	*bus stop*
k	WC umum	11	*internet café (lit. internet stall)*

A popular euphemism for the toilet is **kamar kecil**.

LOCATIONS

belakang	*back*	**depan**	*front*
sebelah	*side*	**samping**	*side*
antara	*between*	**seberang**	*other side*
atas	*above*	**bawah**	*below*
luar	*outside*	**dalam**	*inside*

NEW EXPRESSIONS

numpang tanya ...	*may I ask ...*
bagaimana cara	*what is the method, how does one*
begini	*like this*
pertama	*first, firstly*
belok	*to turn*
lalu, kemudian	*then*
lampu merah	*red light*, (coll.) *traffic light*
terus	(*continue*) *onwards*
lurus	*straight*
persimpangan	*intersection*
terakhir	*last, finally*
repot	*busy, overburdened*

 Conversation 1

09.02 *Ian asks Wibowo for some directions.*

1 Where does Ian want to go?

Ian	Numpang tanya, di mana kedutaan Inggris?
Wibowo	Kedutaan Inggris di alun-alun kota, di antara kantor polisi dan kantor pos.
Ian	Saya tidak ada peta. Alun-alun jauh dari sini?
Wibowo	Oh, tidak. Tidak jauh. Alun-alun dekat. Anda bisa jalan kaki ke sana.
Ian	Bagaimana cara jalan kaki ke sana?
Wibowo	Caranya begini, Anda harus ambil Jalan Adipati. Pertama, keluar hotel dan belok kanan. Lalu, jalan kaki terus sampai lampu merah kedua. Belok kiri di persimpangan itu dan terus lurus sampai Anda masuk alun-alun. Anda akan lihat kedutaannya di seberang alun-alun.
Ian	Jadi terakhir saya harus menyeberang alun-alun?
Wibowo	Ya, betul.
Ian	Di lampu merah kedua ada apa?
Wibowo	Ada apa ya? Oh, ada gereja Katolik. Kalau tidak salah, nama gerejanya Santa Maria.

kanan	*right*
kiri	*left*
keluar	*exit* (v.)
masuk	*enter*

2 **Match the Indonesian word to its opposite, then complete the English translations.**

a	dekat	**1**	kanan	_____
b	pertama	**2**	jauh	_____
c	kiri	**3**	salah	_____
d	betul	**4**	terakhir	_____

3 **Read or listen again and answer the questions.**

   a What does Ian not have?

   b What places are to the left and right of where Ian wants to go?

   c What street should Ian take to get to the square?

   d What is at the second traffic light?

4 **09.03 Now listen to the lines from the conversation and repeat. Be sure to pay attention to the pronunciation.**

 Language discovery

1 **Look at the sentences from the conversation. Put the words in English into Indonesian.**

   a (*How do I*) jalan kaki ke sana?

   b Jalan kaki terus sampai lampu merah (*second*).

   c Anda akan lihat kedutaannya (*across*) alun-alun.

1 GETTING DIRECTIONS

Instead of asking for the **arah jalan** (*street direction*), many Indonesians will ask for **cara naik mobil** (*the way to go by car*) or **cara jalan kaki** (*the way to walk*) to where they are going. Sometimes people omit the mode of travel if it is obvious. The question word **bagaimana** (*how*) is used as you're asking for a method instead of a direction, so that **bagaimana cara** means *how does one* or loosely, *how do I* do something.

Bagaimana cara naik mobil ke Blok M?

How does one go by car to Blok M?

Bagaimana cara ke bandara dari sini?

How does one (go by car) to the airport from here?

2 ORDINAL NUMBERS

Using the **ke–** prefix transforms cardinal numbers into ordinal numbers such as **kedua** (*second*), **ketiga** (*third*) etc. The exception is **pertama** (*first*).

3 TALKING ABOUT LOCATIONS

When you describe where one thing is in relation to another, you should use **di** (*at/in/on*) before the second location. In some cases, for example, with a location such as **seberang** (*other side*), it allows you to say **di seberang** (*across*). In other cases, **di** (*at/in/on*) is simply necessary.

Kantor pos di seberang jalan dari warnet.

The post office is across the street from the internet café.

Mobil saya di belakang kantor.

My car is behind the office. My car is at the back of the office.

Kamar kecil di dalam. Saya tunggu Anda di luar.

The toilet is inside. I wait for you outside.

When using **kiri** (*left*) or **kanan** (*right*), you'd say, for example, **di sebelah kiri** or **di samping kiri** to mean *on the left side of*.

 Practice

1 **Put the following questions into Indonesian.**
   a How does one go to the train station?
   b How does one get to the carpark?
   c How does one walk to the bank from here?

2 **Match the Indonesian to the English.**
   a pertama   1 fourth
   b keenam   2 first
   c keempat   3 sixth

 3 09.04 **Describe the places on your local high street or in your neighbourhood in relation to one another.**

 Pronunciation

 09.05 **Indonesians sometimes omit or drop an *e* sound that comes after a consonant and before a syllable that begins with the letter *r*. Listen to how the following words are pronounced, first with the *e* included and then with the *e* omitted, and repeat.**

1 seberang
2 menyeberang
3 perahu
4 terima kasih

Speaking

 09.06 **Read the questions below and prepare response that are true for you. Then, listen and respond in real time.**

Di mana halte bus yang paling dekat?

Bagaimana cara pergi ke tempat kerjamu dari rumahmu?

 Conversation 2

09.07 *Linda is at the mall, looking for the bathroom.*

1 What is on the right side of the cinema?

Linda	Permisi, kamu tahu di mana kamar kecil yang paling dekat?
Eva	Di lantai tiga.
Linda	Bagaimana cara pergi ke sana?
Eva	Kamu bisa naik eskalator, lift, atau tangga ke lantai tiga. WC umum di depan warnet.
Linda	Aku tidak tahu di mana warnet.
Eva	Warnet di samping kanan bioskop.
Linda	Maaf. Aku kurang tahu di mana itu.
Eva	Mari, aku antar kamu ke sana.
Linda	Tidak usah, terima kasih. Aku akan cari sendiri.
Eva	Tidak apa-apa. Aku juga perlu pergi ke atas.
Linda	Terima kasih. Maaf, aku merepotkan kamu.
Eva	Tidak apa-apa. Mari ikut aku.

lantai	floor, level
tangga	staircase
tidak usah	no need to
sendiri	oneself

While you have used the words **naik** and **turun** to talk about riding and getting on or off a mode of transport, they also mean respectively ascend and descend.

2 Find the expressions in the conversation that mean:

   a How do I get there? _____
   b I don't quite know where that is. _____
   c There is no need to, thank you. _____
   d Come follow me. _____

3 Check, then cover up your answers and see if you can say them without looking at the conversation.

4 Read or listen again and answer the questions.

   a Where is the nearest lavatory?
   b How can Linda get upstairs?
   c What help does Eva offer her?
   d What does Eva need to do?

5 09.08 **Now listen to the lines from the conversation and repeat. Then listen to Eva's lines and respond as Linda.**

Language discovery

1 Look at the sentences from the conversation. Put the words in English into Indonesian.

   a Di (*third floor*).
   b (*I*) akan cari (*myself*).
   c (*No need to*), terima kasih.

1 NUMBERING AND NAMING FLOORS

In Indonesian, a **lantai** (*floor, level*) is not designated as first or second. Instead, **lantai satu** or **L1** is *floor one* meaning the *first floor*, which coincidentally is the *ground floor*, following American convention. The *second floor* is **lantai dua** or **L2**, and so on.

2 DOING SOMETHING ON YOUR OWN

The word **sendiri** (*oneself*) can be used after a verb to say that someone is doing something on his or her own.

Saya pergi sendiri. Dia mau cari sendiri.

I am going by myself. She wants to look for it on her own.

3 ACCEPTING AND REFUSING AN OFFER OF HELP

The phrase **tidak usah** (*no need to*) is often considered the opposite of the word **harus** (*must*). When someone offers to help you or do something for you, you can use **tidak usah** to say that there is *no need* for them to do it. It is also considered good manners to apologise for **merepotkan** (*imposing on, overburdening*) someone when accepting an offer of help.

Terima kasih, tetapi Anda tidak usah mengantar saya.

Thank you, but you do not need to escort me.

Maaf, saya merepotkan Anda.

Sorry, I am imposing on you.

 ## Practice

1 Put the following phrases into Indonesian.
   a first (*or* ground) floor
   b second floor

2 Put the following sentences into English.
   a Saya makan sendiri.
   b Aku akan pulang sendiri.

 3 09.09 **Practise accepting and refusing an offer to escort you somewhere.**

 ## Listening

| tanya | *ask, enquire* | **awas** | *beware (of)* |
| **licin** | *slippery* | **dilarang** | *forbidden* |

1 09.10 **Justin gets lost whilst driving. Listen to the dialogue and answer the following questions.**

    a Why does the woman tell Justin to park his car?
    b Why does she tell him to be careful?
    c What does the woman tell Justin he does not have to do?

The word **hati–hati** (carefully) can also mean be careful.

2 09.11 **Listen to the audio and match the places described to the locations on the map.**

apotek, kantor pos, rumah makan, warnet, apartemen, kantor polisi, alun-alun

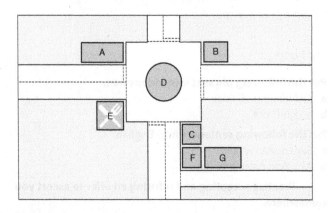

Reading and writing

1 Match the street signs to the relevant situations.
    a trying to park in the afternoon
    b driving down a mountain pass
    c trying to cross the street
    d wanting to drop someone off

1 awas jalan licin

2 dilarang berhenti di sini

3 dilarang parkir 08:00-18:00

4 dilarang menyeberang

2 **Write a text to your friends with directions to your favourite restaurant from the bus stop.**

> Teman-teman, turun bus di halte bus di depan ...

Go further

1 **Match the Indonesian to the English**

a	lantai atas	**1**	*roundabout*
b	lantai bawah	**2**	*intersection, crossroad*
c	pertigaan	**3**	*upper floor*
d	perempatan	**4**	*T-junction*
e	bundaran	**5**	*lower floor*

A *T-junction* is called a **pertigaan** because it is where **tiga** (*three*) paths meet, dividing the area into thirds. Similarly, the **perempatan** (*crossroad*) is where **empat** (*four*) paths meet, dividing the area into quarters. In a multi-storey building, the *upper floors* and *lower floors* are respectively **lantai-lantai atas** and **lantai-lantai bawah.** In a lift, **LB** often marks the levels below ground.

> The **bundaran HI** (*Hotel Indonesia roundabout*) is a famous Jakarta landmark frequently featured in films set in the city.

2 Give the English for the following.
   a Aku turun eskalator pelan-pelan.
   b Kamu menyeberang cepat-cepat.
   c Ibu Dewi parkir hati-hati.
   d Tolong ulang pelan-pelan.

In Indonesian, some adverbs or words describing the way an action is done, such as **pelan-pelan** (*slowly*) and **cepat-cepat** (*quickly*), are created by doubling an adjective such as **pelan** (*slow*) and **cepat** (*quick*). As in English, adverbs can come before or after the verb so that **hati-hati parkir** means *careful whilst parking* and **parkir hati-hati** means *park carefully*.

> When someone is leaving or a party is breaking up, **Hati-hati, ya?** (*Be careful, all right?*) is often used in Indonesia as a goodbye to the one who will be journeying home or elsewhere.

3 09.12 **Read the questions below and prepare responses that are true for you. Then, listen and respond in real time. Do this as many times as you need to for it to become second nature.**

Bagaimana cara mengeja nama Anda?

Bagaimana cara pergi ke bandara dari rumah Anda?

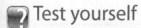

Test yourself

1 Put the words in English into Indonesian.

(*How does one*) pergi ke masjid dari sini? (*Turn*) kiri dan jalan (*onwards*) sampai (*red light*), lalu (*turn right*) di (*intersection*). Kemudian (*cross*) jalan.

2 Use the words in the box to recreate the phrases below.

> kedua, terakhir, anak, pertama, orang, halte

a first (bus) stop
b last person
c second child

3 Match the Indonesian to the English.

a	di bawah	**1**	*behind*
b	di antara	**2**	*across*
c	di belakang	**3**	*below*
d	di sebelah	**4**	*in front of*
e	di depan	**5**	*between*
f	di seberang	**6**	*next to*

4 Complete the sentences using the correct word.

a Tempat parkir di lantai *bawah / salah*.
b Loket karcis di lantai *dua / kedua*.
c Ibu bekerja di lantai *sebelah / atas* stasiun kereta.

5 Give the English for the following.

a Saya tinggal sendiri.
b Mereka berjalan-jalan sendiri di Tebing Tinggi.
c Maria pergi sendiri ke bandara.

6 Give the Indonesian for the following.

a Come, I will escort you.
b There is no need to, thank you.
c Sorry, I am imposing on you.

SELF CHECK

I CAN ...

- ask for and understand directions
- understand sequences using words and numbers
- accept or refuse an offer of help
- recognise warnings
- ask and explain how to do something

10 Semoga cepat sembuh!

Get well soon!

In this unit you will learn how to:
▶ *talk about health complaints and parts of the body.*
▶ *tell others how often you do something.*
▶ *talk about time periods in relation to the present.*
▶ *give and understand negative commands.*
▶ *request appointments.*

CEFR: *Can follow short, simple directions.* **(A1)**; *Can describe habits, past activities and personal experiences.* **(A2)**

Health

When you **berlibur** (*are on vacation*) in tropical Indonesia, you'll probably have to watch your **kesehatan** (*health*) by being careful about the heat, sun, and humidity while your **badan** (*body*) adjusts. Having health insurance is uncommon in Indonesia and residents who are **takut** (*afraid of, nervous about*) becoming ill will try to avoid consuming food and drinks **sembarangan** (*carelessly*). If you **merasa tidak enak badan** (*feel unwell*), you can go to the pharmacy for over-the-counter **obat-obat** (*medicines*) or see a medical professional and obtain a **resep obat** (*drug prescription*). Most small communities benefit from access to a **puskesmas** (*public health clinic*) operated by doctors and **mantri-mantri** (*paramedics*) employed by the government. In larger communities, there are doctors who **praktik** in private clinics, sometimes attached to their homes, and at the **rumah sakit** (*hospital*). It is common for a doctor to offer and attend **janji-janji** (*appointments*) in several locations. This could mean a longer waiting time for a **pasien** if the doctor has to travel through unexpectedly bad traffic that day. If you cannot wait, perhaps because you fear you've **menderita patah tulang** (*suffered a bone fracture*), you can go to the **UGD** or **Unit Gawat Darurat** (*Emergency Unit*).

What do you think **praktik** and **pasien** mean in English?

Vocabulary builder

 10.01 Look at the words and phrases and complete the English translations. Then listen to the recording and imitate the pronunciation of the speakers.

HEALTH

luka	*wound, cut, injury*
sakit	*be ill, be sick, ache, hurt, pain*
sakit kepala	*(have a) headache*
kepala	_____
sakit perut	*(have a) stomach ache*
perut	_____
sakit tenggorokan	*(have a) sore throat*
tenggorokan	_____
sakit kulit	*(have a) skin ailment*
kulit	_____
dokter gigi	*dentist*
gigi	_____
dokter umum	*general practitioner*
dokter anak	_____

MEDICAL PROCEDURES

periksa	*to examine*
diperiksa	*to be examined*
ronsen	*x-ray*
dironsen	*to be x-rayed*
operasi	_____
dioperasi	*to be operated on*

NEW EXPRESSIONS

ada	*to be present (somewhere)*
kenapa	*why*
karena	*because*
jatuh	*fall (down)*
sebaiknya	*it is best that ...*
jangan	*do not (imperative)*
khawatir	*worry*
lupa	*forget*
kali	*(number of) times/occasions*

TIME

sejak	*since*
sampai	*until*
mulai	*to start*
sebelum	*before*
sesudah	*after*
lalu	*past*
depan	*ahead*
lusa	*day after tomorrow*

FREQUENCY

selalu	*always*
sering	*often*
biasanya	*usually*
jarang	*rarely*
tidak pernah	*never*

OTHER PARTS OF THE BODY

muka	*face*
telinga	*ear*
hidung	*nose*
mulut	*mouth*
leher	*neck*
bahu	*shoulder*
lengan	*arm*
siku	*elbow*
pergelangan tangan	*wrist*
tangan	*hand*
jari	*finger*
ibu jari	*thumb*
dada	*chest*
punggung	*back*
pinggul	*hip*
kaki	*leg*
lutut	*knee*
mata kaki	*ankle*
jari kaki	*toe*

10.02 **Listen to the words about time, frequency, and other parts of the body and imitate the pronunciation of the speakers.**

Conversation 1

 10.03 *Linda arrives at a local doctor's practice where a nurse greets her.*

1 What is the matter with Linda?

Linda	Permisi. Pak Dokter ada?
Perawat	Pak Dokter sedang praktik di rumah sakit.
Linda	Sampai kapan Pak Dokter berada di sana?
Perawat	Dia berada di sana sampai jam enam. Ada apa, Bu? Kenapa cari Pak Dokter?
Linda	Karena saya mau minta janji dengan dia. Saya sakit kepala. Leher saya sakit juga. Saya ingin diperiksa oleh Pak Dokter.
Perawat	Sejak kapan kepala dan leher Ibu sakit?
Linda	Sejak mingu lalu. Sesudah saya jatuh pada hari Minggu sewaktu saya berlibur.
Perawat	Sejak tiga hari yang lalu, ya? Ada luka?
Linda	Tidak. Tidak ada luka.
Perawat	Sebaiknya Ibu diperiksa hari ini. Saya rasa Ibu perlu dironsen tetapi Pak Dokter akan lebih tahu.
Linda	Suster bisa buatkan janji untuk saya?
Perawat	Ya, Bu. Jangan khawatir. Saya akan menelpon rumah sakit dan meminta janji untuk Ibu.

oleh	*by*
rasa	*sense, feel*
lebih tahu	*know more/ better*
kadang-kadang	*sometimes*

> A respectful way to address or refer to a doctor is to call him or her **Pak Dokter** or **Bu Dokter**. A **perawat** (*nurse*) is often called a **Suster** (*Sister*) due to the history of missionary service.

2 Find the expressions in the conversation that mean:

a What's the matter, Madam? _____

b Because I want to book an appointment with him. _____

c It is best that you're examined today. _____

3 Read the text or listen again and answer the questions.
   a Is the doctor at the clinic?
   b How long has Linda been in pain?
   c What procedure does the nurse feel Linda will need?

4 10.04 Now listen to the lines from the conversation and repeat. Be sure to pay attention to the pronunciation.

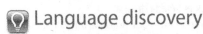 Language discovery

1 Look at the sentences from the conversation. Put the words in English into Indonesian.
   a Saya (*have a headache*). Leher saya (*hurts*) juga. Saya ingin (*be examined by*) Pak Dokter.
   b Pak Dokter (*available*)? Dia (*is*) di sana sampai jam enam.
   c Sejak (*last week*), pada hari Minggu. Sejak tiga hari (*ago*), ya?
   d (*After*) saya jatuh pada hari Minggu sewaktu saya berlibur.
   e (*Since*) kapan kepala dan leher Ibu sakit?

1 MEDICAL AILMENTS AND APPOINTMENTS

You've seen the word **sakit** (*ill, ache, hurt, pain*) used in Unit 3 so that **dia sakit** means *she was ill*. Here are its other uses.

Saya sakit gigi.	*I have a toothache.*
Gigi saya sakit.	*My tooth hurts.*
Saya merasa sakit.	*I feel ill* or *I feel pain.*

The word **luka** (*wound*) can be used in two ways.

Kaki saya luka.	*My leg is wounded.*
Ada luka di kaki saya.	*There is a wound on my leg.*

When you're discussing your medical ailments and treatments, the focus of conversation is you, your body, and how your body is the object of actions. In Indonesian, the focus of the sentence comes first. In medical situations, the passive voice is thus used frequently. For example, **saya dioperasi oleh dokter** (*I was operated on by the doctor*) is heard more frequently than **dokter mengoperasi saya** (*the doctor operated on me*).

An *appointment* with a doctor is a **janji** (lit. *promise*) and you would say, for example, **saya mau minta janji dengan dokter** (*I want to book/request an appointment with the doctor*).

2 MORE ON THE VERB ADA

Recall that the word **ada** can be used to mean *to be available*. In this sense, it can also mean *to be present* somewhere. When the location is stated, you should use the **ber-** form, **berada**.

Apakah dokter ada?

Is the doctor in? Is the doctor available?

Dokter Umar berada di rumah sakit.

Dokter Umar is (present) at the hospital.

3 PAST AND FUTURE TIME PERIODS

When you want to talk about specific days, weeks, months, and years, you can mention the time and describe how it is related to the present using **lalu** (*past*), **depan** (*ahead*), and **akan datang** (*will come*). There is also a particular word **lusa** that means *the day after tomorrow*.

tiga tahun yang lalu	*three years ago*
minggu lalu	*last week*
dua hari yang lalu	*two days ago*
lusa	*the day after tomorrow*
tiga hari yang akan datang	*three days from now*
minggu depan	*next week*
dua bulan yang akan datang	*two months from now*

4 BEFORE AND AFTER

When you want to talk about events happening before or after a particular time period, you can use the words **sebelum** (*before*) or **sesudah** (*after*) as you would their English counterparts.

Kapan saya harus kembali? Seminggu sebelum operasi.

When must I return? A week before the operation.

Kapan aku akan diperiksa? Sesudah kamu dironsen.

When will I be examined? After you are x-rayed.

5 TALKING ABOUT WHEN SOMETHING BEGINS AND ENDS

You can use the word **sejak** (*since*) with time phrases to talk about when something began. However, if the beginning of the event is in the future, use **mulai dari** (*starting from*) instead.

Sejak kapan kamu demam? Sejak dua hari yang lalu.

Since when have you had the fever? Since two days ago.

Mulai dari kapan dia berlibur? Mulai dari minggu depan.

Starting from when is he on vacation? Starting from next week.

To talk about when an event ended or will end, you can use the word **sampai** (*until*).

Sampai kapan lutut kamu sakit? Sampai minggu lalu.

Until when did your knee hurt? Until last week.

Sampai kapan dokter berada di sana? Sampai nanti sore.

Until when will the doctor be there? Until later this afternoon.

 Practice

1 **Put the following sentences into English.**
   a Punggung saya sakit.
   b Lengan dan siku saya luka.

2 **Complete the sentences with** *ada* **or** *berada*.
   a Maaf, Pak Dokter tidak. Saya berbicara dengan siapa?
   b Kapan Anda di Indonesia?

3 **Put the following sentences into Indonesian.**
   a She was x-rayed three months ago.
   b You will be operated on next week.

4 **Choose the correct word.**
   a sesudah dioperasi   *before / after* being operated on
   b sebelum minum obat   *before / after* taking the medicine

 5 **10.05 Read the questions below and prepare responses that are true for you. Then, listen and respond in real time.**
   a Sejak kapan Anda belajar bahasa Indonesia?
   b Mulai dari kapan Anda berlibur?

 Pronunciation

 10.06 You might hear *kh* **pronounced similarly to** *ch* **in the English word** *loch* **or as the letter** *k*. **Listen to how the following words are pronounced and repeat.**

1 khas   2 khitanan

3 khawatir   4 khusus

Speaking

 10.07 You are a patient phoning the doctor's to make an appointment. Prepare your responses to the following questions. Then, listen and respond in real time.

Resepsionis	Bisa saya bantu?
Pasien	*Say you want to book an appointment with your chosen medical professional*
Resepsionis	Untuk hari apa?
Pasien	*Make a choice to suit your schedule*
Resepsionis	Saya bisa buatkan janji untuk sore hari. Anda bisa datang pada jam berapa?
Pasien	*Make a choice to suit your schedule*

Conversation 2

 10.08 *Jon is being examined by a doctor.*

1 What does the doctor tell Jon not to do?

Dokter	Sejak kapan Pak Jon merasa tidak enak badan?
Jon	Sejak dua hari yang lalu. Saya sakit perut dan muntah setiap hari.
Dokter	Anda sering atau jarang harus pergi ke WC?
Jon	Saya sering harus pergi ke WC.
Dokter	Apakah Anda selalu makan hati-hati?
Jon	Tidak selalu. Saya kadang-kadang makan sembarangan. Dan saya sering lupa makan.
Dokter	Sesudah ini, tolong jangan makan sembarangan. Ini resep obat antibiotik. Anda harus minum obat ini tiga kali sehari. Obatnya harus diminum sampai habis.
Jon	Di mana saya bisa membeli obatnya?
Dokter	Anda bisa menebus resepnya di apotek.

muntah	to vomit
tebus	to redeem
habis	depleted, all gone

2 Find the expressions in the conversation that mean:
   a take this medicine _____
   b antibiotic drug prescription _____
   c buy the medicine _____
   d redeem the prescription _____

3 Check, then cover up your answers and see if you can say them without looking at the conversation.

4 Read or listen to the text again and answer the following questions.
   a Since when has Jon been feeling ill?
   b What symptoms does Jon have?
   c What are Jon's eating habits?
   d Where can Jon get the prescription?

5 10.09 Now listen to the lines from the conversation and repeat. Then listen to the doctor's lines and respond as Jon.

 Language discovery

1 Look at the sentences from the conversation. Put the words in English into Indonesian.
   a Anda harus minum obat ini (*three times a day*).
   b Sesudah ini, (*do not*) makan sembarangan.
   c Dan saya (*often forget to eat*).

1 HOW MANY TIMES ...?

Whenever you saw the phrase **sekali lagi** (*once more*) perhaps you had the idea that **sekali** could be another way of saying **satu kali** (*one time*). That would be correct! To say *three times a day*, you would therefore say **tiga kali sehari**. The question you'd ask is **Berapa kali sehari?** (*How many times a day?*)

2 DON'T ...

To tell people to not do something, use the word **jangan** (*do not*). You can also say **tolong jangan** (*please do not*).

Jangan makan sembarangan. *Don't eat carelessly.*

Tolong jangan khawatir. *Please don't worry.*

3 TALKING ABOUT HABITS USING FREQUENCY WORDS

You can talk about how rarely or often you do something by using a frequency word such as **jarang** (*rarely*) or **sering** (*often*), which you place before the verb. When you negate the combination, place **tidak** (*not*) before the combination.

Kamu sering sakit? *Are you often ill?*

Tidak. Aku tidak sering sakit. *No. I'm not often ill.*

 Practice

1 **Give the Indonesian sentences for the following.**
   a I practise at the hospital twice a week.
   b My leg is examined four times a year.

2 **Unscramble the words to make full sentences.**
   a janji lupa dokter Tolong Anda dengan jangan!
   b makan dironsen Anda sebelum Jangan.

 3 **10.10 Read the questions below and prepare responses that are true for you. Then, listen and respond in real time.**
   a Kamu sering berlibur?
   b Anda biasanya makan di mana?

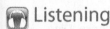 Listening

kecelakaan	*accident, (coll.) have an accident*
ambulans	*ambulance*
Tidak ada apa-apa.	*Nothing's the matter.*
Semoga cepat sembuh.	*Get well soon.*

1 **10.11 Ani has returned from the public health clinic after receiving treatment for a minor accident. Ani's mother is worried about her. Listen to the dialogue and answer the following questions.**
   a What did Ani do that was unusual, according to her mother?
   b Where is she injured and did she need an x-ray?
   c When does Ani have to return to the clinic?

2 **10.12 Listen to the patients being interviewed and match the names to the ailments. Then, listen again and respond by wishing him/her a speedy recovery in real time.**

a **Tuti**   *toothache*

b **Ian**   *hip bone fracture*

c **Siti**   *influenza*

> From what you know about the word **perawat** (*nurse*), you may have recognised that to **rawat** others is to *nurse* or *care for* them. If you see signs for **rawat inap** and **rawat jalan** in an Indonesian hospital, you would also be correct in thinking they mean, respectively, *inpatient care* and *outpatient care*.

 ## Reading and writing

 1 **Anisa has written an email to Owen after hearing that he was in hospital. Read her email.**

Owen,

Apa kabar? Mary menelpon aku tadi malam dari Amerika. Dia bilang kamu kecelakaan dan menderita patah tulang bulan lalu, kemudian kamu dirawat inap di rumah sakit selama dua minggu. Dia juga bilang sesudah itu, kamu boleh pulang, tetapi kamu harus kembali ke rumah sakit sekali seminggu untuk diperiksa oleh dokter dan dirawat jalan. Bahu kamu masih sakit? Semoga cepat sembuh, Owen! Aku tunggu kabarmu.

Salam hangat,
Anisa

2 **Imagine your friend is recovering from an illness or injury. Write an email to wish him or her a speedy recovery.**

Go further

Here are some other useful words:

hamil	*to be pregnant*
kursi roda	*wheelchair*
sakit flu	*(have) the flu*

When you saw **tidak pernah** (*never*) used to talk about habits, you probably also considered the meaning of **pernah**.

1 Put the following into English. Think carefully.
  a Saya tidak pernah belajar.
  b Saya pernah belajar bahasa Indonesia.

One of the words used in Indonesian to discuss when things happened, **pernah** is used to talk about whether something has *ever* happened before so that in a sentence **pernah** can be thought of as *have ... before*.

Saya pernah sakit flu.	I have had the flu before.

Native speakers also use **belum pernah** to mean *have never yet* and **sudah pernah** to mean *already have ... before*.

Saya belum pernah hamil.	I've never yet been pregnant.
Saya sudah pernah hamil.	I've already been pregnant before.

If you want to say, for example, that you (*never have the flu*) because influenza never troubles you, you would say you **tidak pernah sakit flu**. However, if you want to say that you *have never yet had the flu before* in your lifetime, you would say you **belum pernah sakit flu.**

When people know you are studying Indonesian, they are more likely to ask if you **sudah pernah pergi ke Indonesia** (*have already gone to Indonesia before*) than to ask if you **pernah pergi ke Indonesia** (*have gone to Indonesia before*) because there is an expectation that you have already made a trip there or that you'll be making a trip there if you haven't yet done so.

2 10.13 Read the questions below and prepare your own responses. Then, listen and respond in real time.
  a Sampai kapan kamu belajar bahasa Indonesia?
  b Kamu kadang-kadang perlu kursi roda?
  c Kamu sudah pernah berlibur di Indonesia?

Test yourself

1 Put the words in English into Indonesian.

Tahun lalu, sepupu saya (*had a stomach ache*). Dia (*requested an appointment with*) dokter. Dia (*was examined by*) dokter. Ibu Dokter memberikan dia (*drug prescription*). Dia (*took that medicine*) dan (*felt*) lebih baik. (*Since*) itu, dia makan hati-hati.

2 Unscramble the words to make full sentences.
   a puskesmas berada Mantri-mantri di .
   b ada Dokter Bu ?

3 Match the Indonesian phrases to the English.
   a dua minggu yang lalu   **1** *two weeks from now*
   b minggu depan   **2** *two weeks ago*
   c dua minggu yang akan datang   **3** *next week*

4 Put the following sentences into English.
   a Tolong minum obat sesudah makan malam.
   b Mata kaki saya sakit sebelum saya dioperasi.

5 Choose the correct word.
   a sampai tahun lalu   *until / since* last year
   b sejak saya jatuh   *until / since* I fell down

6 Put the following sentences into Indonesian.
   a How many times a week?
   b Drink this medicine two times a day.

7 Complete the sentences to give negative commands.
   a _____ takut. Ini tidak sakit.
   b _____ _____ lupa belajar bahasa Indonesia.

8 Put the words in English into Indonesian.
   a Keluarga Thomas (*are often on vacation*) di Kanada.
   b Pasien-pasien (*are never examined*) bersama.
   c Jari-jari Affandi (*are always hurting*).

SELF CHECK

I CAN ...

- ○ talk about health complaints and parts of the body
- ○ tell others how often I do something
- ○ talk about time periods in relation to the present
- ○ give and understand negative commands
- ○ ask for appointments.

1 **Put the following everyday expressions into Indonesian.**
   a What time is it now?
   b Which one is the next train?
   c Is there a table for eight people?
   d Enjoy your meal.
   e The cheque, please.
   f May I ask …
   g How do I walk to the supermarket?
   h Please repeat slowly.
   i Sorry that I am imposing on you.
   j Don't forget.

2 **Match the questions and statements to the replies.**

   a Berapa ongkos perjalanan?   1 Selamat tinggal.
   b Berapa lama perjalanan?   2 Tidak ada apa-apa.
   c Selamat jalan.   3 Tiga puluh ribu rupiah.
   d Silakan duduk.   4 Tidak usah.
   e Saya antar Anda ke sana.   5 Enam jam.
   f Ada apa?   6 Terima kasih.

3 **Pingkan keeps a travel journal. Read the entry about her recent trip home and answer the following questions.**

Malam ini dingin. Aku naik bus dari Batu lalu ganti kendaraan di Malang. Kereta jurusan Surabaya berangkat dari stasiun pada jam setengah tujuh. Harga tiketnya empat puluh ribu. Sesudah dua jam duduk di dalam kereta, aku sampai di Surabaya. Di stasiun tidak ada ojek jadi aku naik taksi dan terkena macet. Aku terlambat tetapi makan malam di rumah orang tuaku masih hangat. Aku rasa ibuku tahu aku akan terlambat. Minggu depan aku harus kembali ke Batu tetapi minggu ini aku akan bermain bersama keponakan-keponakanku dan makan masakan ibu.

a Was the night warm or cold?

b What time did the train leave and how long was the trip?

c What transport option was and was not available in Surabaya?

d Where did Pingkan have dinner and how was the food?

e When does she have to return to Batu?

4 Match the Indonesian to the English.

a	dilarang parkir	**1**	*do not stop here*
b	dilarang menyeberang	**2**	*beware of slippery pavement*
c	awas trotoar licin	**3**	*no parking*
d	jangan berhenti di sini	**4**	*do not walk here*
e	jangan berjalan di sini	**5**	*no crossing*

5 Give the following in English.

a jam tujuh kurang seperempat pagi

b jam dua lewat sepuluh menit siang

c semangkok bubur ayam

d segelas es kopi susu

e satu botol air mineral

f pasien ketujuh

6 Ian and Tini are at a street stall. She's picking up a takeaway while he's having a drink and waiting for his food. Read their conversation and answer the following questions.

Ian	Tini, kamu pesan apa untuk dibawa pulang?
Tini	Aku pesan empat porsi sate ayam, dua porsi lontong, dan dua porsi nasi goreng udang pedas.
Ian	Kamu bisa makan semua makanan itu?
Tini	Ini pesanan keluargaku dan kami lapar.
Ian	Oh begitu. Mereka suka makanan yang pedas, ya? Aku suka yang pedas juga. Aku baru pesan mie rebus pedas dan ayam bakar lada hitam.
Tini	Ayam bakarnya enak. Kamu minum apa?
Ian	Ini es susu kedelai manis. Kamu mau coba?
[Ian motions for the vendor to come over.]	
Ian	Pak, satu es susu kedelai manis lagi!
Tini	Tidak usah, Ian, terima kasih.
Ian	Tidak apa-apa, Tini. Cobalah.
Tini	Berapa, Pak? Aku mau bayar sendiri.

a What did Tini order and why did she order so much food?
b What kind of food does Ian like?
c What did Ian just order to eat and what does Tini say about it?
d What does Ian order after getting the vendor to come over?
e Who is paying for Tini's drink?

7 Unscramble the words to make complete sentences.

a tanah beralergi Saya kacang.
b kamar ke mengantar Dia saya kecil.
c garpu ambilkan Tolong.
d suka tidak yang Saya asin.
e mau umum Saul janji dokter dengan minta.

8 Look at the English translations, then choose the correct word to complete the Indonesian phrases.

a tidak *asam / asin*   not salty
b saya *haus / kenyang*   I am thirsty
c *kecap / saos* manis   sweet soy sauce
d *lusa / lalu*   the day after tomorrow
e tahun *lusa / lalu*   last year

9 Pak Rusli has taken notes about a house that he's thinking of moving to with his family. Complete his notes by putting the words in English into Indonesian.

- (*not far*) dari bandar udara
- ada (*police station*) yang (*near*)
- ada (*crosswalk*) di setiap (*traffic light*)
- ada halte bus (*across the street from*) sekolah
- di mal ada (*internet café on the 3rd floor*)
- rumah (*between*) rumah sakit dan kantor
- (*on the upper floor*), kamar tidur (*next to*) ruang duduk
- ada halaman besar (*in front of*) rumah

10 Give the root of the words in parentheses.

   a Kamu belum pernah makan (makanan) Indonesia?

   b Dokter (memeriksa) saya karena saya sakit tenggorokan.

   c Dia (dioperasi) dua minggu yang akan datang.

   d Tolong hati-hati kalau Anda (merasa) pusing.

   e Dokter (menekan) pergelangan tangan saya.

11 Choose the correct word.

   a *Sejak / Belum* kapan kamu tinggal di Indonesia?

   b *Sudah / Sampai* kapan Anda berada di sana?

   c Mulai *dari / ke* kapan Jon berlibur di Inggris?

   d Berapa *kali / kalian* sebulan?

   e *Kalian / Kali* mau minum apa?

12 Bima has written an e-mail to Ian's parents describing their son's life as a boarder in his house. Complete the excerpt by putting the words in Indonesian into English.

---

1 (*YTH*) Mr and Mrs Webb,

2 (*Empat bulan yang lalu*), your son Ian 3 (*mulai*) studying at the university. Ian 4 (*selalu*) studies hard. He 5 (*kadang-kadang*) forgets to eat. He 6 (*jarang*) sleeps early. When I asked him 7 (*kenapa*) he studies so hard, he laughed and said it's 8 (*karena*) he 9 (*tidak pernah*) knows when to stop. Ian 10 (*merasa tidak enak badan*) this week 11 (*jadi*) he 12 (*minta janji dengan dokter*), who said 13 (*Ian sakit flu*). Every day, our 14 (*kedua*) and youngest child shouts into Ian's room, '15 (*Semoga cepat sembuh!*)' and hugs him 16 (*sebelum*) she goes to school. We doubt this is the cure but it certainly pleases your son and 17 (*dia minum obat dua kali sehari*) so that his 18 (*kesehatan*) improves. I will write to you again 19 (*tiga hari yang akan datang*) to give you an update. I also want to ...

---

13 *Selamat ulang tahun, Pak Budi!* **Budi has given Jon directions to get to his 50th birthday party. Match the sentences to the English translations.**

   a Caranya begini, pertama, turun bus di Jalan Kenanga.

   b Masuk jalan itu dan jalan kaki terus selama kira-kira lima menit sampai Jalan Merak.

c Kalau Anda tidak bisa lihat nama jalannya, di persimpangan Jalan Kenanga dan Jalan Merak ada klinik dokter gigi.

d Belok kiri di persimpangan itu. Kemudian jalan terus.

e Belok kanan sesudah masjid.

f Terakhir, cari nomor delapan puluh delapan.

1 Turn right after the mosque.

2 If you can't see the street name, at the intersection of Kenanga Street and Merak Street there is a dental clinic.

3 The method is this, first, get off the bus at Kenanga Street.

4 Finally, look for number eighty-eight.

5 Turn left at that intersection. Then continue walking.

6 Enter that street and continue walking for roughly five minutes until Merak Street.

Grammar guide

Here are a few fundamental grammar points that you can review whenever you need to get your bearings:

Word order

The word order in Indonesian sentences does not differ much from the word order in English sentences. For example, **saya makan jeruk** (*I eat an orange*) and **jeruk dimakan oleh saya** (*the orange was eaten by me*). However, an Indonesian noun phrase is the reverse of what an English noun phrase would be so that *my left foot* would be **kaki kiri saya**. Depending on word order, moreover, a pronoun such as **saya** (*I*) can also work as a possessive such as *my* so that **topi saya** is *my hat*. Verbal phrases are in the same order as they are in English so that *not still sleeping* would be **tidak masih tidur.**

Words

Some Indonesian words share the same beginnings and endings. This is because Indonesian words can be developed out of root words using affixes (whether prefixes, suffixes, or both), which are word parts attached to the beginning or end of a word. Here are some affixes and examples of their use:

▶ –an is a suffix used to form a noun so that **makan** (*to eat*) becomes **makanan** (*food*)
▶ ber– is a prefix used to form an active verb so that **main** (*to play*) becomes **bermain** (*play*) and **sepeda** (*bicycle*) becomes **bersepeda** (*cycle, ride a bicycle*)
▶ di– is a prefix used to form a passive verb so that **periksa** (*to examine*) becomes **diperiksa** (*to be examined*)
▶ meX–, where X stands for a consonant that changes depending on the first letter of the root word, is a prefix used to form an active verb so that **periksa** (*to examine*) becomes **memeriksa** (*examine*). In

general meX–verbs are used when the action involves someone or something else. For example, you **mendengar** (*hear*) a sound and you **memeriksa** (*examine*) a patient

▶ pe– or peX– are prefixes that are used to make an actor out of a verb or action word so that a **pekerja** (*worker*) is someone who **kerja** (*works*)

Questions

You can form Indonesian questions in the way you would form statements or in the way you would form questions in English. A question can be posed as **Apa ini?** (*What is this?*) or as **Ini apa?** (*This is what?*), which has the same word order as the statement **Ini topi.** (*This is a hat.*) In a question that is ordered like a statement, the question word, in this case **apa** (*what*) is placed where the unknown information would be in the answer. Any question involving numbers must be asked using **berapa** (*how many*), whether the answer is a date, a time, or an amount.

Situating actions in time

Verbs do not change according to when actions happen since there are no tenses in Indonesian. To situate an action in time, use words and phrases such as **tadi** (*earlier*), **nanti** (*later*), **jam tiga sore** (*three p.m.*), **kemarin** (*yesterday*), **hari ini** (*today*), **besok** (*tomorrow*), and so on. You can also use temporal markers to say, for example, whether an action **pernah** (*ever*) happened or **akan** (*will*) happen. Here are some other markers:

baru	*recently, just*	**masih**	*still*
belum	*not yet*	**sudah**	*already*

Location

Whenever something or someone *is* somewhere, you must use the location word **di** (*at/in/on*). For example, **dia duduk di sini** (*he sits here*) and **dia bermain di luar** (*she plays outside*).

Counting

Indonesian speakers might use classifiers when counting things so that, for example, people are counted in **orang**, animals are counted in **ekor**, and large things are counted in **buah**. You say **dua orang anak** (*two children*) when counting with classifiers and **dua anak** (*two children*) when counting without them.

References

Sneddon, J.N. (2010) *Indonesian: A Comprehensive Grammar* 2nd Edition. London: Routledge.

Stevens, A.M. & Schmidgall-Tellings A.Ed. (2004) *A Comprehensive Indonesian-English Dictionary*. Athens: Ohio University Press.

Answer key

Unit 1

Indonesian
Europe, Japan, telephone, university, accountant, doctor

VOCABULARY BUILDER

Greetings
morning, afternoon, evening

CONVERSATION 1

1 Jakarta
2 a 4 Where do you live?, **b 3** Excuse me., **c 1** Until we meet again.
d 2 Where do you come from?
3 a between 3pm and 6pm, **b** Liverpool, **c** University of Palembang,
d colleague

LANGUAGE DISCOVERY

1 a Ini Jonathan Curtis. Saya Budi., **b** Di mana Anda bekerja? Saya kerja di
universitas., **c** Dari mana Anda berasal? Anda tinggal di mana?

PRACTICE

1 a Bahasa Inggris bahasa ibu saya., **b** Saya bekerja di kantor., **c** Ini kolega
saya., **d** Utomo tinggal di Cina.
2 a 3 kerja, **b 1** temu, **c 4** asal, **d 2** bahasa
3 Model answers:
a Saya berasal dari India., **b** Saya tinggal di Korea., **c** Saya bekerja di hotel di
Skotlandia., **d** Nama bank saya Bank Indonesia.

SPEAKING

Model answers:
a Saya Patricia Smith., **b** Kenalkan. Ini Wati., **c** Kolega saya berasal dari
Malaysia.

CONVERSATION 2

1 Hotel Indonesia
2 a Siapa nama kamu?, **b** Apa itu?, c Terima kasih., **d** Sama-sama.
3 a Siti, **b** England, **c** Linda, **d** informal
4 Hotel Indonesia., Sama-sama., Dah, Bu Linda!

LANGUAGE DISCOVERY

1 a Siapa, **b** apa

PRACTICE

1 a Siapa nama Anda/kamu?, **b** Apa nama universitas itu?
2 Model answers:
Kamu orang apa, Chris?, Aku orang Kanada. Dan kamu?, Aku orang
Australia., Orang apa kamu, Peter?, Aku orang Singapura.

LISTENING

1 a 3 01:30 p.m., **b 4** 05:00 p.m., **c 2** 06:00 a.m., **d 1** 11:00 p.m.
2 Heryanto, Indonesia, Scotland, University of Aberdeen, Mimi, USA,
England, University of London
3 Model answers:
a Nama aku James., **b** Aku tinggal di Selandia Baru sekarang., **c** Aku berasal
dari Hong Kong.

READING AND WRITING

1 a Alex orang Indonesia., **b** Alex berasal dari Sulawesi., **c** Alex tinggal di
Cardiff sekarang., **d** Alex bekerja dan belajar di Universitas Wales.

GO FURTHER

1 a 5 Javanese, **b 3** Sundanese, **c 4** Malay, **d 1** Madurese, **e 2** Batak
2 Model answers:
a Pramoedya Ananta Toer orang Jawa. Pramoedya Ananta Toer orang
Indonesia., **b** Saya/Aku belajar bahasa Indonesia.

TEST YOURSELF

1 a 2 11:00 a.m., **b 3** 04:00 p.m., **c 1** 08:00 a.m.
2 a Where do you work?, **b** I work at a bank., **c** Bambang works in Japan.
3 a di, b dari, c ke
4 a Siapa, **b** Apa, **c** Siapa
5 a Saya/aku orang Wales., **b** Kolega saya orang Selandia Baru., **c** Anda
orang apa?

Unit 2

COMMUNITY
1 bermain sepak bola

VOCABULARY BUILDER
Adjectives
old, short

CONVERSATION 1
1 They went scuba diving.
2 a Saya tetangga baru Anda., **b** Siapa dia?, **c** Dia senang apa?, **d** Ayo!
3 a evening, **b** no, **c** Linda and Affandi, **d** introduce Affandi to Linda.

LANGUAGE DISCOVERY
1 a teman lama saya, **b** Kita, Kami **c** bukan, tidak

PRACTICE
1 a my new acquaintance, **b** our short friend
2 a Kita, **b** Kami.
3 Model answers:
a Apakah Anda berlatih pencak silat di Indonesia? Tidak. Saya tidak berlatih pencak silat di Indonesia., **b** Apakah Anda orang Indonesia? Bukan. Saya bukan orang Indonesia., **c** Apakah Anda tinggi? Tidak. Saya tidak tinggi.

SPEAKING
Model answers:
Dia Julia. Dia orang Inggris. Dia tinggi. Kami senang berenang, bermain bulu tangkis, dan makan-makan.
Dia Arthur. Dia orang Amerika. Dia pendek. Kami senang menari di kampung, membaca, dan minum-minum.

CONVERSATION 2
1 081174625329
2 a 3 earlier this morning, **b 4** now, **c 2** later this afternoon, **d 1** later tonight
3 a earlier this morning, **b** later tonight, **c** later this afternoon, **d** daytime (between 10a.m. and 3p.m.)
4 Nomor ponsel saya kosong – delapan – satu – satu – tujuh – empat – enam – dua – lima – tiga – dua – sembilan., Ya. Itu nomor ponsel saya., Sampai nanti sore.

LANGUAGE DISCOVERY

1 a tadi pagi, **b** Berapa, Pak Jon

PRACTICE

1 a Saya bermain musik tradisional tadi pagi dan tadi malam., **b** Dia bermain bulu tangkis nanti sore.

2 Model answers:

Berapa nomor telpon Anda? Nomor telpon saya kosong – dua – tujuh – tiga – lima – tiga – empat – delapan – kosong – sembilan., Berapa nomor telpon Rachel? Nomor telpon saya nol – delapan – satu – satu – enam – empat – dua – lima – tiga – tujuh – lima.

LISTENING

1 a in the school yard, **b** on the porch, **c** later this evening

2 HP: 07798681434, kantor 041390572, rumah 0419903416.

3 Model answers:

a Tidak. Teman saya tidak muda. Dia tua., **b** Saya harus membaca sekarang., **c** Nomor telpon aku tujuh-nol-tujuh-lima-nol-satu-sembilan.

READING AND WRITING

1 Model answer:

Halo dari Indonesia! Eko teman baru saya. Dia orang Indonesia. Dia berasal dari Ponorogo. Kami bertemu di universitas. Dia belajar bahasa Inggris dan saya belajar bahasa Indonesia. Dia ramah dan pendek. Tadi pagi kami belajar di rumah dia. Sampai nanti!

GO FURTHER

1 a Saya senang., **b** Bermain gamelan menyenangkan., **c** Saya senang pergi ke Indonesia.

2 Model answers:

a Ya. Musik tradisional negara saya menyenangkan., Tidak. Musik tradisional negara saya tidak menyenangkan., **b** Ya. Bertemu orang Indonesia menyenangkan., Tidak. Bertemu orang Indonesia tidak menyenangkan.

TEST YOURSELF

1 a Dia tetangga baru saya, **b** Ini nomor telpon sekolah dia., **c** Itu teras rumah saya.

2 a Kita, **b** Kami, **c** Kita

3 a Tidak, tidak, **b** tidak, **c** Bukan, bukan

4 a 2 earlier this afternoon, **b 3** later this afternoon, **c 4** last night, **d 1** later this evening

5 a number, **b** cell phone, **c** What is your hand phone number?
6 a Ke mana aku dan Linda pergi sekarang?, **b** Di mana dia bertemu Linda?, **c** Linda dan dia berselam skuba di mana?

Unit 3

FAMILY

1 keluarga-keluarga

VOCABULARY BUILDER
Family members
younger siblings, older siblings, grandchildren

CONVERSATION 1

1 Jon
2 a Kasihan!, **b** Apa kabar?, **c** Bagus!, **d** Apa kabar keluarga Anda?
3 a early afternoon, **b** Budi's wife, **c** three, **d** Jon's elder brother's family.

LANGUAGE DISCOVERY

1 a baik, **b** baik, **c** Bagus
2 a Saya belum menikah., **b** Mereka sudah punya cucu-cucu.

PRACTICE

1 a How are you?, **b** I am well.
2 a Sudah. Saya sudah menikah., Belum. Saya belum menikah. **b** Sudah. Saya sudah punya cucu., Belum. Saya belum punya cucu.

SPEAKING

Model answers:
Siti dan Harmoko orang tua Ina. Edwin kakek Rudi. Mutia nenek Ratna. Ina ibu Rudi dan Bastian. Lina dan Ratna anak-anak perempuan Hendri dan Ina. Rudi, Bastian, Lina, dan Ratna cucu-cucu Edwin dan Mutia. Bastian saudara laki-laki Lina. Ratna saudara perempuan Rudi. Hendri suami Ina. Ina istri Hendri.

CONVERSATION 2

1 Jon's younger brother
2 a Jon was still working, **b** two, **c** repeat one more time, **d** that Budi will call Jon tomorrow

3 a 4 Can I speak to Mr Jon?, **b 3** I don't understand., **c 2** Can I leave a message?, **d 1** All right.
4 Saya tidak mengerti. Tolong ulang sekali lagi., Saya mengerti sekarang. Apa pesan Anda?, Baiklah., Sama-sama.

LANGUAGE DISCOVERY

1 a Saya menelpon dia besok., **b** dua adik, **c** Tolong bilang, 'Saya mengerti sekarang.'

PRACTICE

1 a Saya menelpon kakak laki-laki saya kemarin., **b** Saya menelpon adik perempuan saya besok.
2 a anak, **b** kantor-kantor
3 Model answers:
Bisa titip pesan?, Apa pesan Anda?, Tolong bilang, 'Kita belajar bahasa Indonesia hari ini', Baiklah. Nanti saya sampaikan., Terima kasih., Sama-sama.

LISTENING

1 a yes, **b** yes, **c** her husband's parents' house.
2 grandfather and grandmother are going to Jakarta later this afternoon, grandmother
3 Model answers:
a Kabar baik., **b** Mereka baik., **c** Ya. Saya mengerti sedikit bahasa Indonesia.

GO FURTHER

1 Model answers:
a Tidak. Saya tidak punya banyak saudara., Ya. Saya punya banyak saudara.,
b Bisa. Saya bisa bicara bahasa Indonesia., Bisa. Sedikit.

TEST YOURSELF

1 a Apa kabar?, **b** Kabar baik. Dan Anda?, **c** Saya baik juga., **d** Bagus!
2 a 3 already married, **b 1** not yet married, **c 2** still married
3 a belum, hari ini, **b** sudah, kemarin, **c** Besok
4 a rumah-rumah, **b** enam anak, **c** sembilan keluarga
5 a say, **b** understand, **c** Please repeat once more., Please repeat one more time.

R1

1 a Selamat pagi, **b** Selamat siang, **c** Selamat sore, **d** Selamat malam

2 a saya, aku, **b** Anda, kamu, **c** dia, **d** kita, kami, **e** mereka

3 a Terima kasih., **b** Sama-sama., **c** Permisi., **d** Sampai bertemu lagi., **e** Bisa bicara dengan Ibu Linda?

4 a siapa, **b** Dari mana, **c** Di mana, **d** Apa, **e** ke mana

5 a Ini, bekerja (*or* kerja), **b** Itu, tinggi, teman, orang Inggris, bahasa Indonesia, **c** senang, **d** tetangga baru Linda, orang Indonesia, kenal

6 a Bukan. Dia bukan orang Selandia Baru., **b** Tidak. Mereka tidak berlatih pencak silat tadi siang., **c** Tidak. Anak saya tidak gemuk.

7 a 5 I don't understand., **b 1** Please repeat once more., **c 4** Can I leave a message?, **d 3** What is your message?, **e 2** I will pass it on.

8 a What is Anisa's (*or* your) phone number?, **b** My phone number is seven-two-five-six-zero-four-one-nine., **c** I have eight children. My children live in Solo., **d** How many are your siblings (*or* How many siblings do you have)?, **e** My siblings are three in number (*or* I have three siblings).

9 a sudah belajar tadi pagi, **b** masih bekerja nanti, **c** belum punya anak

10 a 3 Kabar baik., **b 4** Bagus!, **c 2** Kasihan!, **d 1** Tolong bilang …

11 a Suteja's younger brother Koes, **b** his grandparents, his cousin, and himself, **c** yesterday, **d** played Sundanese traditional music with his grandfather on the porch

Unit 4

DAILY LIFE

1 makan siang

VOCABULARY BUILDER

Days of the week
Friday, Sunday
Numbers
30, 31, 90, 99

CONVERSATION 1

1 At the weekend

2 a Thursday, **b** She is a civil servant, **c** sixteen years old, **d** Yes

3 a 4 Hari ini hari Kamis., **b 3** Sampai nanti!, **c 2** Tidak apa-apa., **d 1** Dia pergi pada hari Selasa.

4 Hari ini hari Kamis., Oh, tidak apa-apa. Apa pekerjaan dia?, Kapan dia pergi?, Siapa memasak di rumah minggu ini?, Oh begitu. Berapa umur anak Pak Frans?, Oh ya, Pak Frans sudah makan siang?, Baiklah. Sampai nanti!

LANGUAGE DISCOVERY

1 a Kapan, setiap, **b** akan, **c** makan malam, makan malam, **d** Berapa

PRACTICE

1 a Kapan kamu menonton televisi?, **b** Saya akan pulang pada hari Jum'at., **c** Setiap hari Minggu saya belajar bahasa Indonesia dan memasak makan siang.
2 a I will shop tomorrow., **b** I will listen to the radio., **c** I will study tonight.
3 a Saya makan siang di rumah setiap hari., **b** Budi makan pagi pada akhir minggu., **c** Jon memasak makan malam setiap malam.
4 Model answers:
Berapa umur Anda? Umur saya empat puluh satu tahun.
Berapa umur ibu Anda? Ibu saya berumur enam puluh tujuh tahun.
Berapa umur adik Anda? Umur adik saya dua puluh sembilan tahun.

SPEAKING

Model answers:
Nani mandi dan pergi ke kantor pada hari Senin. Dia pulang dan memasak makan malam pada hari Selasa. Pada hari Rabu dia makan siang di kantor. Pada hari Kamis dia pergi ke bank dan tidur. Pada hari Jum'at dia makan siang di rumah orang tua dia. Nani menonton televisi dan mandi pada hari Sabtu. Dia belajar bahasa Inggris pada hari Minggu.

CONVERSATION 2

1 She is an engineer.
2 a At a foreign company., **b** Twenty-eight years old., **c** She has to go to sleep., **d** Sleep well *or* Have a good sleep
3 a 2 a company, **b 1** an employee, **c 4** an engineer, **d 3** a servant

LANGUAGE DISCOVERY

1 a I work at a foreign company., **b** I am an engineer.

PRACTICE

1 a ekor, **b** buah, **c** orang, **d** buah
2 Model answers:

Apa pekerjaan Anda? Saya seorang pegawai di perusahaan Telindo. Dan Anda? Saya seorang akuntan, Apa pekerjaan kamu? Aku manajer di hotel. Dan kamu?

LISTENING

1 Monday – **7** woke up and ate breakfast at home, Tuesday – **1** went to the bank, Wednesday – **4** ate lunch at the office, Thursday – **5** called Jon, Friday – **3** went to the mosque, Saturday – **2** cooked in the kitchen, Sunday – **6** helped the children do their homework
2 Model answers:
a Hari ini hari Senin., **b** Saya mendengarkan radio pada hari Rabu., **c** Saya seorang pegawai negeri.

GO FURTHER

1 a 3 meneliti, research, **b 4** belajar, study, **c 1** melukis, paint, **d 2** menari, dance
2 Model answers:
Dia seorang ilmuwan., Dia seorang perawat.

TEST YOURSELF

1 a Kapan, **b** setiap Selasa malam, **c** pada hari Jum'at, **d** pada hari Senin.
2 a I shall help mother shop on Saturday., **b** They will bathe tomorrow night., **c** I will do my homework on Sunday.
3 a makan pagi, **b** memasak makan siang, **c** makan malam
4 a 2 He is fifteen years old., **b 3** She is thirty years old., **c 1** He is seventy years old.
5 a delapan orang anak, **b** sembilan belas orang pegawai negeri, **c** dua puluh empat buah televisi, **d** seorang pekerja LSM
6 a pekerjaan, **b** bekerja, **c** pelajar

Unit 5

SHOPPING

1 toko batik

VOCABULARY BUILDER

Shopping
credit card, discount

CONVERSATION 1

1 Two hundred thousand rupiah
2 a Cobalah., **b** Tolong tunggu sebentar., **c** Silakan bayar di kasir.
3 a black, **b** 41, **c** he has to pay in cash

LANGUAGE DISCOVERY

1 a yang itu, yang biru, **b** Tolong, Silakan, **c** sepatu yang lebih murah,
d ukuranmu, Ukuranku, **e** harganya

PRACTICE

1 a Yang mana yang paling murah?, **b** Saya ambil yang ini.
2 a Tolong, **b** Silakan
3 a Those shorts are too large., **b** These socks are not long enough.
4 a Ukuran kemejaku enam belas., **b** Roknya hijau dan rokmu abu-abu.
5 Model answers:
Berapa harga ponsel Anda? Harga ponsel saya dua juta rupiah., Berapa
harga topimu? Harganya seratus ribu rupiah., Berapa harga pasta gigimu?
Harga pasta gigiku lima puluh ribu rupiah.

SPEAKING

Model answers:
a Saya berbelanja di pusat perbelanjaan., **b** Tidak. Kalau di Indonesia, saya
tidak berbelanja di ruko. Saya berbelanja di mal., **c** Ukuranku tiga puluh
enam.

CONVERSATION 2

1 A toothbrush
2 a 2 the dark blue one, **b** 4 a twenty-thousand rupiah note,
c 1 ten thousand exactly, **d** 3 change
3 a (light) green and (dark) blue, **b** toothpaste, **c** twenty thousand rupiah,
d yes
4 Saya suka warna hijau dan warna biru tua., Saya ambil yang biru tua.
Berapa harganya?, Tidak. Terima kasih. Saya tidak mau beli pasta gigi
hari ini.

LANGUAGE DISCOVERY

1 a mau beli, **b** ada, Ada **c** hijau muda, biru tua

PRACTICE

1 a boleh lihat, yang merah, **b** mau pergi, warung

2 a Sorry. I don't have exact change., **b** The cell phone is still available, sir, and there is a twenty-percent discount!

3 Model answers:

Sendal saya putih. Kaos saya abu-abu. Celana pendek saya coklat tua., Ponsel saya kuning. Komputer saya hitam. Jas saya coklat muda.

LISTENING

1 a It is large., **b** It is being sold cheaply., **c** Three hundred million rupiah.

2 biru, enam setengah, Tidak ada, pasar swalayan, dijual, pasar swalayan, toserba

READING AND WRITING

1 Ira's.

GO FURTHER

1 a sembilan ratus lima puluh rupiah, **b** empat ribu dua ratus rupiah, **c** dua belas ribu sembilan ratus rupiah, **d** tujuh ratus lima puluh ribu rupiah, **e** satu juta enam ratus dua puluh lima ribu rupiah

2 a 5 pharmacy, **b 1** electronics shop, **c 4** craft and art market, **d 2** copy shop, **e 3** bookshop

3 Model answers:

a Saya mau membeli oleh-oleh di pasar seni., **b** Saya paling suka warna abu-abu., **c** Harga belanjaan sehari-hari saya lima puluh ribu rupiah., **d** Di kota saya, aspirin dijual di apotek.

TEST YOURSELF

1 a Yang mana, **b** yang itu, **c** yang ini

2 a Tolong, **b** Silakan

3 a 2 not cheap enough, **b 3** largest, **c 1** too long

4 a This is not my size., **b** Your size is nine and a half., **c** Its/her/his size is too small.

5 a Berapa harga rok pendek yang coklat?, **b** Harganya dua ratus dua puluh ribu rupiah.

6 a mau pergi, **b** boleh coba

7 a Tidak ada baju dalam di toko ini., **b** Kami ada kain-kain tradisional.

8 a pink, **b** dark green

Unit 6

ACCOMMODATION

1 saya perlu fasilitas air panas

VOCABULARY BUILDER

double, per night, confirmation

CONVERSATION 1

1 the 30th of May to the 2nd of June
2 a Bisa saya bantu?, **b** Tidak ada., **c** Berapa tarif kamar per malam?
3 a her husband, **b** adjoins the bedroom, bathtub, no shower, **c** 130,000 rupiah per night

LANGUAGE DISCOVERY

1 a lebih suka, daripada, **b** kurang, **c** tanggal berapa, tanggal tiga puluh Mei

PRACTICE

1 a Mereka lebih suka hotel berbintang daripada losmen., **b** Saya lebih suka kamar mandi dengan fasilitas air panas., **c** Dia lebih suka menyewa kamar kos.
2 a Sorry. I don't quite like this room., **b** They do not like that hotel., **c** I don't quite like living at a boarding house.
3 Model answers:
Hari ini tanggal berapa? Hari ini tanggal 27 September.
Tanggal berapa hari ini? Tanggal 4 Januari.

SPEAKING

Model answers:
Di kota Bandung, saya mau menginap di Losmen Tugu. Saya mau menginap dari tanggal tiga Februari sampai tanggal sepuluh Februari. Saya perlu dua kamar. Untuk tiga orang tamu.
Di Desa Mendut, saya mau menginap di Hotel Mataram. Saya mau menginap dari tanggal sembilan belas Februari sampai tanggal dua puluh lima Februari. Saya perlu satu kamar. Untuk dua orang tamu.

CONVERSATION 2

1 She has reserved a double room with air-conditioning, an adjoining bathroom, and internet facilities from the 30th of May to the 2nd of June.

2 a 3 Betul., **b 1** Alamatnya Jalan Lumumba., **c 4** Kembali., **d 2** Belum.
3 a spell her name, **b** no, **c** Jalan Lumumba No. 35 *or* 35 Lumumba Street
4 Alamatnya Jalan Lumumba nomor tiga puluh lima., Bisa. L—U—M—
U—M—B—A.

LANGUAGE DISCOVERY

1 a 1 the address, **b 2** the street name
2 a Di mana alamatnya?, **b** Alamatnya Jalan Lumumba nomor tiga puluh
lima.

PRACTICE

1 a Di mana kamar mandinya?, **b** Siapa tamunya?, **c** Di mana alamatnya?
2 Model answers:
Di mana alamatmu? Alamatku Jalan Queen Anne No. 20.
Di mana alamatnya? Alamatnya Jalan Hollycroft No. 6A.

LISTENING

1 a from the 6th of July to the 8th of July, **b** 2 nights, **c** 40 dollars,
d breakfast
2 Surabaya 03 Juni, Ambon 15 Januari, Manado 08 September, Semarang
17 April, Medan 11 Agustus, Batam 26 Februari, Padang 22 Juli, Jakarta 09
Maret, Makassar 24 Nopember

READING AND WRITING

2 a Marni, **b** Tanggal, **c** JL. Kintamani No. 14, **d** Depok, **e** 16424, **f** (021)650-
0592

GO FURTHER

1 a 6 smoke-free room, **b 3** extra bed, **c 8** baby cot, **d 7** safe, **e 2** iron and
ironing board, **f 1** work desk, **g 4** tea and coffee maker, **h 5** hairdryer
2 Apa arti 'internet gratis' dalam bahasa Inggris?, Artinya 'free internet'., Apa
arti 'unlimited wifi' dalam bahasa Indonesia?, Artinya 'koneksi wifi tanpa
batas'.
3 Model answers:
Di Indonesia, saya menginap di hotel berbintang dan di losmen.
Saya perlu tempat tidur ekstra, brankas, dan kamar bebas rokok.
Keperluan anak saya kolam renang. Keperluan-keperluan orang tua saya
pancuran air mandi dan pembuat teh dan kopi.
Ya. Saya akan mencari kamar kos di Indonesia.

TEST YOURSELF

1 a Dia lebih suka kamar tanpa AC., **b** Budi lebih suka menginap di hotel berbintang., **c** Mereka lebih suka kamar dobel daripada kamar singel.
2 a Saya kurang suka menginap di penginapan., **b** Aku kurang suka menyewa kamar kos., **c** Mereka kurang suka belajar pada akhir minggu.
3 a tanggal berapa, **b** pada tanggal 17 Januari, **c** tanggal 23 September.
4 a Where is the hotel?, **b** How much is the room rate per night?, **c** What is the telephone number?
5 a Di mana, **b** kepada, **c** Jalan.

R2

1 a 3 Thursday, **b 8** Sunday, **c 4** day, **d 2** Friday, **e 6** Tuesday, **f 1** Monday, **g 5** Saturday, **h 7** week
2 a Berapa umur kamu? or Umur kamu berapa?, **b** Kapan kamu mandi?, **c** Kamu cari apa?, **d** Kamu mau beli apa?, **e** Berapa ukuranmu? or Ukuranmu berapa?, **f** Berapa harganya? or Harganya berapa?, **g** Yang mana?, **h** Di mana kamu menginap? or Kamu menginap di mana?, **i** Di mana alamatnya? or Alamatnya di mana?
3 a Selamat tidur., **b** Silakan bayar di kasir., **c** Tolong tunggu sebentar., **d** Belilah., **e** Hari ini hari Rabu, tanggal delapan Agustus.
4 returned home – pulang, go to sleep – pergi tidur, having dinner – makan malam, watching television – menonton televisi, woke up – bangun, bathed – mandi, have breakfast – makan pagi, busy – sibuk, will – akan, at the weekend – pada akhir minggu, in May – pada bulan Mei.
5 a seventeen years, **b** ten people, **c** nine months, **d** (the year) eight hundred and six, **e** one million five hundred thousand rupiah
6 a Anisa's father, **b** a skirt and blazer, **c** red and light yellow, **d** a new cell phone battery and a pair of dark blue sandals, **e** they were not available at the mall
7 a pasang, **b** ekor, **c** orang, **d** buah
8 a Carilah losmen., **b** Tolong bantu saya., **c** Silakan menginap di rumah kami.
9 a Tidak apa-apa., **b** Terima kasih kembali., **c** Yang ini lebih murah., **d** Sampai nanti!, **e** Artinya 'guest'., **f** Maaf. Yang ini tidak dijual.
10 a Berapa tarif kamar per malam pada bulan Maret?, **b** Saya mau memesan kamar dobel., **c** Anda sudah ada reservasi di hotel kami?
11 a a foreign company, **b** housewife, **c** the goods there are the cheapest ones, **d** every Friday, **e** small, **f** an Australian foreign student, **g** in November

12 internet access, air-conditioning, attached bathroom, hot water, shower

13 Tono, at the till there is no change. I don't have exact change. Do you have a fifty-thousand-rupiah note?

14 a Ningsih Suparman, **b** 12 Juli 1980, **c** pekerja LSM, **d** Jalan Sadikin No. 34, **e** Jakarta, **f** 101622, **g** 0215365701

15 a three months, **b** 3 bedrooms, 2 bathrooms, **c** a small kitchen, **d** a large porch and a swimming pool, **e** they can pay it in dollars or rupiah

Unit 7

TRANSPORTATION

1 ongkos perjalanan

VOCABULARY BUILDER

return, one-way

Time

minute

CONVERSATION 1

1 his passport

2 a naik kelas ekonomi, **b** Saya belum tahu., **c** Selamat tinggal.

3 a 3:45pm, **b** an open-date return ticket, **c** one suitcase

LANGUAGE DISCOVERY

1 a naik kelas ekonomi, **b** pada jam empat kurang seperempat sore

PRACTICE

1 a Jon takes a plane to Bali., **b** Ita rode a bicycle to her mother's house., **c** Dimas is travelling by car to the office.

2 a jam dua belas lewat lima belas (*or* lewat seperempat) siang, **b** jam sepuluh kurang sepuluh menit pagi, **c** jam setengah delapan malam

3 Model answers:

Kereta api berangkat pada jam dua belas lewat seperempat siang.

Ferinya akan sampai di Lombok pada jam sepuluh kurang sepuluh pagi.

Saya mau memesan taksi untuk jam setengah delapan malam.

SPEAKING

1 Model answer:

Helen pergi ke kantor naik mobil pada jam tujuh pagi. Dia pergi makan siang naik bus pada jam dua belas siang. Dia kembali ke kantor naik ojek pada jam setengah dua siang. Dia pulang ke rumah naik mobil pada jam lima lewat dua puluh sore.

2 Model answer:

Saya pergi ke universitas naik kereta bawah tanah pada jam sepuluh pagi. Saya pergi makan siang naik taksi pada jam satu siang. Saya pulang ke rumah naik bus pada jam setengah sembilan malam.

CONVERSATION 2

1 twenty five minutes

2 a 3 I'm going to Solo., **b 1** What time is it now?, **c 2** What time is the bus leaving?

3 a the bus to Semarang, **b** at 1:15pm, **c** on the bus or at the ticket booth

4 Ibu bisa naik bus jurusan Semarang di sini., Busnya berangkat pada jam satu lewat seperempat siang., Jam satu kurang sepuluh.

LANGUAGE DISCOVERY

1 a Loketnya di situ., **b** Bus itu baru berangkat., **c** Mau ke mana, Bu?

PRACTICE

1 a Your bus will stop there., **b** How much is the trip fare from here to (over) there?

2 a The aeroplane from Ambon just/recently arrived., **b** He just/recently bought a ticket.

3 Model answers:

Anda mau pergi ke mana? Saya mau pergi ke hotel saya.

Mau ke mana? Mau ke kantor.

LISTENING

1 a 7:00am and 8:00am, **b** two hours, **c** ninety thousand rupiah

2 a travelling to Trawas – **5** by car, **b** going to Madura – **4** by ship, **c** going into the city – **1** by taxi, **d** getting to the market – **3** go on foot, **e** when you have no time – **2** by motorcycle service

3 Model answers:

Sekarang jam setengah lima sore., Saya berangkat dari rumah pada jam tujuh pagi., Saya sampai di kantor kira-kira pada jam setengah sembilan pagi.

GO FURTHER

1 morning, afternoon, evening

2 a Saya sampai (*or* datang) di Indonesia pada malam hari., **b** Saya berangkat pada pagi hari., **c** Saya akan naik kereta bawah tanah pada siang hari., **d** Dia akan datang ke Lembang naik kereta api pada sore hari.

3 Model answers:

Di Jakarta, sekarang pukul sembilan malam WIB., Di London, sekarang pukul dua siang GMT.

Saya datang dari rumah saya., Saya datang dari Inggris.

Ya. Aku mau datang ke rumahmu., Tidak. Aku tidak mau.

Terima kasih. Aku sampai pada pagi hari., Terima kasih! Aku sampai pada jam dua siang.

TEST YOURSELF

1 pesawat/kapal terbang, tiket sekali jalan, Perjalanan, (pergi) naik mobil, naik taksi, naik sepeda motor, naik, jurusan, turun

2 a 3:40pm *or* twenty to four in the afternoon, **b** 7:15am *or* a quarter past seven in the morning, **c** 8:30pm *or* half past eight in the evening, **d** 12:00pm *or* twelve noon

3 a Pada jam berapa kereta jurusan Madiun datang?, **b** Mobil mereka sampai mada jam sebelas malam., **c** Jam berapa Anda mau berangkat?, **d** Jam berapa pesawat berikutnya berangkat?

4 a sini, **b** situ, **c** sana

5 a Saya (*or* Aku) baru kembali dari Gili., **b** Penumpang-penumpang baru turun kapal (*or* pesawat) terbang.

6 b Mau di mana?

Unit 8

CUISINE

1 seporsi (*or* satu porsi) nasi

VOCABULARY BUILDER

Cooking methods

a goreng – **4** to fry *or* fried, **b** rebus – **1** to boil *or* boiled, **c** bakar/panggang – **2** to roast/grill *or* roasted/grilled, **d** kukus – **5** to steam *or* steamed, **e** tumis – **3** to stir-fry *or* stir-fried

Popular menu items

prawn cracker, meat skewer, curry, soup

CONVERSATION 1

1 sweet iced tea, hot tea, iced coffee, cold water without ice
2 a Yang mana yang enak?, **b** Dan ini makanan Anda datang sekarang., **c** Tolong ambilkan saya satu sedotan.
3 a one bowl of egg noodle soup, one glass of iced coffee, and two portions of chicken skewers, **b** a straw, **c** Enjoy your meal

LANGUAGE DISCOVERY

1 a memesan, **b** pesanan, **c** secangkir, **d** yang pedas, pedas

PRACTICE

1 a rebus, boil, **b** goreng, fry, **c** kukus, steam
2 a makanan, food, **b** minuman, drink, **c** masakan, cooking *or* cuisine
3 a Grandfather wishes to order a cup of civet coffee., **b** My younger sister does not want a bowl of chicken soup., **c** They want a portion of soy grilled fish.
4 Model answers:
Saya suka yang tidak pahit. Yang mana tidak pahit?, Saya suka yang asin. Yang mana asin?, Saya suka yang tidak pedas. Yang mana tidak pedas?

SPEAKING

Model answers:
Saya mau meja untuk satu orang.
Saya ingin memesan sepiring nasi goreng ikan asin yang pedas, satu porsi tahu dan tempe, dua potong kue bolu kukus, secangkir kopi luwak manis, dan segelas jus alpukat.

CONVERSATION 2

1 the grilled (*or* roasted) fish
2 a enak sekali, **b** masih lapar, **c** sudah selesai, **d** makan bersama
3 a eatery *or* restaurant, **b** the waiter did not hear him, **c** to clear the table, **d** on Saturday
4 Maaf. Jum'at ini saya akan makan bersama Yati., Sabtu? Bisa. Aku bisa makan bersama kamu pada hari Sabtu.

LANGUAGE DISCOVERY

1 a Yang mana, Yang itu., **b** ada, Ada **c** Berapa harganya

PRACTICE

1 a Father wants another (*or* one more) plate of chicken rice., **b** Three more portions of goat skewers, please.

2 a Tolong ambilkan bon kami., **b** Tolong minta bonnya.

3 Model answers:

Mari makan., Anda mau makan siang bersama saya?, Kamu mau makan bersama?

LISTENING

1 a to be taken away, **b** iced coconut water, **c** rice, fried shrimp, and two fried soybean cakes

2 Model answers:

Saya ingin memesan makanan untuk dibawa pulang. Saya mau satu porsi ayam lada hitam, satu sop tahu, satu porsi lontong, dan satu kepiting asam manis.

Saya mau satu nasi, satu mie, dan dua porsi udang bakar. Tolong dibungkus, ya?

READING AND WRITING

1 Saya tidak bisa makan bersama kalian siang ini tetapi di meja makan ada makanan dan minuman yang enak untuk kalian semua. Ada lontong, nasi, sate kambing, udang rebus, air jeruk, dan jus alpukat. Selamat makan!

GO FURTHER

1 a sumpit – **3** chopsticks, **b** sendok teh – **5** teaspoon, **c** pisau – **1** knife, **d** pisau dapur – **2** kitchen knife, **e** sendok garpu – **4** cutlery

2 soy sauce, sweet soy sauce, chilli sauce

3 Model answers:

a Ya. Saya perlu sendok garpu., Ya. saya perlu sebuah pisau dan sepasang sumpit., **b** Boleh. Saya boleh minum minuman beralkohol., Tidak. Saya tidak boleh minum alkohol. **c** Ya. Saya punya alergi kacang tanah., Tidak. Saya tidak beralergi.

TEST YOURSELF

1 a We will wait for our food., **b** Mr Bejo is wrapping (*or* repackaging) their drinks., **c** I am taking home Leslie's cooking.

2 a Bubur sagu makanan dari Maluku., **b** Babi panggang masakan tradisional di Toba., **c** Kopi luwak minuman mahal.

3 a Saya ingin memesan segelas (*or* satu gelas) air dingin dan dua gelas bir., **b** Istrinya mau makan seporsi (*or* satu porsi) lontong., **c** Anak-anak saya mau satu ikan bakar dan dua mie goreng.

4 a Yang mana tidak asin?, **b** Kalau Anda suka yang manis, cobalah singkong goreng., **c** Anda ingin coba susu kedelai kami?

5 a satu teh lagi, **b** dua porsi nasi lagi

6 a 3 How much is it all?, **b 1** Please fetch the cheque., **c 2** May I ask for the cheque?

7 a bersama, **b** bersama, **c** Mari

Unit 9

FINDING YOUR WAY

1 Saya perlu bantuan

VOCABULARY BUILDER

Places

a kantor pos – **5** post office, **b** kantor polisi – **6** police station, **c** stasiun kereta – **7** train station, **d** halte bus – **10** bus stop, **e** bandara – **9** airport, **f** kedutaan – **3** embassy, **g** warnet – **11** internet café, **h** bioskop – **2** cinema, **i** tempat parkir – **8** parking space/carpark, **j** tempat penyeberangan – **1** crossing/crosswalk, **k** WC umum – **4** public toilet

CONVERSATION 1

1 to the British embassy

2 a dekat – **2** jauh, near – far, **b** pertama – **4** terakhir, first – last, **c** kiri – **1** kanan, left – right, **d** betul – **3** salah, correct – incorrect

3 a a map, **b** police station and post office, **c** Jalan (*or* Street) Adipati, **d** a Catholic church (Santa Maria *or* St. Mary's)

LANGUAGE DISCOVERY

1 a Bagaimana caranya, **b** kedua, **c** di seberang

PRACTICE

1 a Bagaimana caranya pergi ke stasiun kereta?, **b** Bagaimana caranya ke tempat parkir?, **c** Bagaimana caranya jalan kaki ke bank dari sini?

2 a 2 first, **b 3** sixth, **c 1** fourth

3 Model answer:

Bank di sebelah kanan toko buku. Kantor pos di antara apotek dan restoran Nusa Dua. Halte bus di depan gereja. Warnet di belakang bioskop. Kantor polisi di seberang jalan dari bioskop. Apartemen saya di atas supermarket. Tempat parkir di bawah Hotel Lido.

SPEAKING

Model answer:
Halte bus yang paling dekat di depan kantor saya.
Model answer:
Pertama, keluar rumahku dan belok kiri. Jalan terus sampai Jalan Flask. Kemudian belok kanan di persimpangan itu dan jalan kaki sampai stasiun kereta Hampstead. Naik kereta bawah tanah sampai stasiun Euston. Turun di situ, lalu ganti kereta. Naik kereta jurusan Victoria sampai stasiun Charing Cross. Turun di sana dan keluar stasiun. Terakhir, belok kiri.

CONVERSATION 2

1 the internet café
2 a Bagaimana caranya pergi ke sana?, **b** Aku kurang tahu di mana itu., **c** Tidak usah, terima kasih., **d** Mari ikut saya.
3 a on the third floor, in front of the internet café, **b** Linda can take the escalator, lift, or stairs, **c** Eva offers to escort her there, **d** Eva needs to go upstairs
4 Tidak usah, terima kasih. Aku akan cari sendiri., Terima kasih. Maaf, aku merepotkan kamu.

LANGUAGE DISCOVERY

1 a lantai tiga, **b** Saya, sendiri, **c** Tidak usah

PRACTICE

1 a lantai satu, **b** lantai dua
2 a I eat by myself, **b** I will go home on my own.
3 Model answers:
Tidak usah, terima kasih. Saya akan cari sendiri., Terima kasih. Maaf, saya merepotkan Anda.

LISTENING

1 a It is forbidden to park where he is going., **b** The pavement is slippery., **c** He does not need to walk quickly.
2 a kantor polisi, **b** apotek, **c** kantor pos, **d** alun-alun, **e** rumah makan, **f** warnet, **g** apartemen

READING AND WRITING

1 a 3 dilarang parkir 08:00-18:00, **b 1** awas jalan licin,
c 4 dilarang menyeberang, **d 2** dilarang berhenti di sini
3 Model answer:
Teman-teman, turun bus di halte bus di depan apotek. Belok kiri dan
masuk Jalan Gunawarman. Jalan lurus terus sampai persimpangan jalan itu
dan Jalan Rusa. Belok kanan. Restorannya di seberang jalan dari bank.

GO FURTHER

1 a lantai atas – **3** upper floor, **b** lantai bawah – **5** lower floor, **c** pertigaan –
4 T-junction, **d** perempatan – **2** intersection or crossroad, **e** bundaran –
1 roundabout
2 a I go down the escalator slowly., **b** You cross quickly., **c** Mrs Dewi parks
carefully., **d** Please repeat slowly.
3 Model answers:
Caranya mengeja nama saya begini, W—A—N—T—A—G—E.
Caranya begini, dari rumah saya, pergi ke stasiun kereta bawah tanah.
Kemudian naik kereta bawah tanah ke Stasiun Paddington dan ganti
kereta di sana. Naik kereta jurusan Heathrow dan turun di bandara
Heathrow.

TEST YOURSELF

1 Bagaimana caranya, Belok, terus, lampu merah, belok kanan,
persimpangan or perempatan, menyeberang
2 a halte pertama, **b** orang terakhir, **c** anak kedua
3 a 3 below, **b 5** between, **c 1** behind, **d 6** next to, **e 4** in front of, **f 2** across
4 a bawah, **b** dua, **c** atas
5 a I live by myself., **b** They walked about on their own in Tebing Tinggi., **c**
Maria went by herself to the airport.
6 a Mari, saya antar Anda., **b** Tidak usah, terima kasih., **c** Terima kasih. Maaf,
saya merepotkan Anda.

Unit 10

HEALTH

1 praktik – practice, pasien – patient

VOCABULARY BUILDER

Health

kepala – head, perut – stomach, tenggorokan – throat, kulit – skin, gigi –
teeth, dokter anak – paediatrician

Medical procedures
operasi – operation

CONVERSATION 1
1 she has a headache and her neck hurts
2 a Ada apa, Bu?, **b** Karena saya mau minta janji dengan dia., **c** Sebaiknya
Ibu diperiksa hari ini.
3 a no, **b** three days, **c** she will need to have an x-ray taken

LANGUAGE DISCOVERY
1 a sakit kepala, sakit, diperiksa oleh, **b** ada, berada, **c** minggu lalu, yang
lalu, **d** Sesudah, **e** Sejak

PRACTICE
1 a My back hurts/aches, **b** My arm and elbow are wounded.
2 a Maaf, Pak Dokter tidak ada. Saya berbicara dengan siapa?, **b** Kapan
Anda berada di Indonesia?
3 a Dia dironsen tiga bulan yang lalu., **b** Anda/Kamu akan dioperasi
minggu depan.
4 a after, **b** before
5 Model answers:
a Sejak empat bulan yang lalu., **b** Mulai dari hari Senin saya berlibur.

SPEAKING
Model answers:
Saya mau minta janji dengan dokter anak., Untuk hari Rabu. Saya bisa
datang pada jam setengah lima sore.

CONVERSATION 2
1 he tells Jon not to eat carelessly after this
2 a minum obat ini, **b** resep obat antibiotik, **c** membeli obatnya,
d menebus resepnya
3 a since two days ago, **b** stomach ache, vomiting, going to the toilet
often, **c** he sometimes eats carelessly and he often forgets to eat, **d** at the
pharmacy
4 Saya sering harus pergi ke WC., Tidak selalu. Saya kadang-kadang makan
sembarangan. Dan saya sering lupa makan.

LANGUAGE DISCOVERY

1 a tiga kali sehari, **b** jangan, **c** sering lupa makan.

PRACTICE

1 a Saya praktik di rumah sakit dua kali seminggu., **b** Kaki saya diperiksa empat kali setahun.

2 a Tolong jangan lupa janji Anda dengan dokter!, **b** Jangan makan sebelum Anda dironsen.

3 Model answers:

Tidak. Saya tidak sering berlibur. Saya jarang berlibur., Saya biasanya makan di warung.

LISTENING

1 a she rode a motorcycle carelessly, **b** on her face and nose but she didn't need a x-ray, **c** two weeks from now

2 a 2 hip bone fracture, **b 3** influenza, **c 1** toothache

Model answer:

Semoga cepat sembuh, Siti!, Semoga cepat sembuh!, Semoga cepat sembuh, Ibu Tuti!

READING AND WRITING

1 Zadie, apa kabar? Aku dengar sejak minggu lalu kamu tidak enak badan. Apakah kamu sudah merasa lebih baik hari ini? Semoga cepat sembuh! Salam hangat, Maggie

GO FURTHER

1 a I never study., **b** I have studied Indonesian (language) before.

2 Model answers:

a Sampai bulan depan., Sampai saya selesai., **b** Ya. Saya kadang-kadang perlu kursi roda., Tidak. Saya tidak pernah perlu kursi roda., **c** Sudah. Saya sudah pernah berlibur di Indonesia., Belum. Saya belum pernah berlibur di Indonesia.

TEST YOURSELF

1 sakit perut – had a stomach ache, minta janji dengan – request an appointment with, diperiksa oleh – was examined by, resep obat – drug prescription, minum obat itu – took that medicine, merasa – felt, Sejak – Since

2 a Mantri-mantri berada di puskesmas., **b** Bu Dokter ada?, **c** Siapa berada di kamar tunggu?

3 a 2 two weeks ago, **b 3** next week, **c 1** two weeks from now
4 a Please take the medicine after dinner., **b** My ankle hurt before I was operated on.
5 a until, **b** since
6 a Berapa kali seminggu?, **b** Minum obat ini dua kali sehari., **c** Pak/Bapak Budi pergi ke dokter tiga kali setahun.
7 a Jangan, **b** Tolong, jangan
8 a sering berlibur, **b** tidak pernah diperiksa, **c** selalu sakit

R3

1 a Jam berapa sekarang? or Sekarang jam berapa?, **b** Yang mana kereta berikutnya? or Kereta berikutnya yang mana?, **c** Ada meja untuk delapan orang?, **d** Selamat makan. **e** Tolong bonnya., **f** Numpang tanya ...,
g Bagaimana cara jalan kaki ke pasar swalayan (or supermarket)?, **h** Tolong ulang pelan-pelan, **i** Maaf, saya/aku merepotkan Anda/kamu., **j** Jangan lupa.
2 a 3 Tiga puluh ribu rupiah., **b 5** Enam jam., **c 1** Selamat tinggal.,
d 6 Terima kasih., **e 4** Tidak usah., **f 2** Tidak ada apa-apa.
3 a cold, **b** 6:30p.m., two hours, **c** the motorcycle service was not available, the taxi was available, **d** her parents' house, the food was still warm,
e next week
4 a 3 no parking, **b 5** no crossing, **c 2** beware of slippery pavement,
d 1 do not stop here, **e 4** do not walk here
5 a 6:45a.m., **b** 2:10p.m., **c** a bowl of chicken porridge, **d** a glass of iced milk coffee, **e** one bottle of mineral water, **f** the seventh patient
6 a four portions/orders of chicken skewers, two portions/orders of steamed rice cake, two portions/orders of spicy prawn fried rice, because her family is hungry, **b** spicy food, **c** spicy noodle soup, black pepper roasted/grilled chicken, she says the chicken is delicious, **d** another sweetened iced soy milk, **e** Tini herself
7 a Saya beralergi kacang tanah., **b** Dia mengantar saya ke kamar kecil.,
c Tolong ambilkan garpu., **d** Saya suka yang tidak asin. or Saya tidak suka yang asin., **e** Saul mau minta janji dengan dokter umum.
8 a asin, **b** haus, **c** kecap, **d** lusa, **e** lalu
9 tidak jauh – not far, kantor polisi – police station, dekat – near, tempat penyeberangan – crosswalk, lampu merah – traffic light, di seberang jalan dari – across the street from, warnet di lantai tiga – internet café on the 3rd floor, di antara – between, di lantai atas – on the upper floor, di sebelah – next to, di depan – in front of

10 a makan, **b** periksa, **c** operasi, **d** rasa, **e** tekan
11 a Sejak, **b** Sampai, **c** dari, **d** kali, **e** Kalian
12 1 Dear, **2** Four months ago, **3** started, **4** always, **5** sometimes, **6** rarely, **7** why, **8** because, **9** never, **10** felt unwell, **11** so/therefore, **12** asked for an appointment with the doctor, **13** Ian has the flu, **14** second, **15** Get well soon!, **16** before, **17** he takes the medicine twice a day, **18** health, **19** three days from now
13 1 c, **2** f, **3** b, **4** e, **5** a, **6** d

Indonesian–English glossary

Here is a list of all the Indonesian vocabulary included in this book. The Indonesian words have been listed alphabetically. To get you started on how Indonesian dictionaries work, words that have also been presented in root form are only listed in root form unless there is a difference in meaning. For example, **bekerja** (*work*) is only listed as **kerja** (*work*) but **ambil** (*to take*) and **ambilkan** (*to fetch*) are separate entries.

abu-abu	*grey*	anak tiri	*stepchild*
ada	*there is/are, has/have,*	Anda	*you, your*
	to be available, to be	angkat	*to lift (up), clear* (coll., v.)
	present (somewhere)	angklung	*bamboo musical*
Ada apa?	*What's the matter?*		*instrument*
Apa kabar?	*How are you?*	antar	*escort*
adik	*younger sibling*	antara	*between*
Agustus	*August*	antibiotik	*antibiotic*
air	*water*	antiseptik	*antiseptic*
air jeruk	*orangeade*	apa	*what*
akan	*will, going to, shall*	Apakah	*(interrogative in yes/no*
akhir	*end* (n.)		*questions)*
akomodasi	*accommodation*	apakah	*whether, if*
aku	*I, me, my*	api	*fire*
akuntan	*accountant*	apotek	*pharmacy*
alamat	*address*	April	*April*
alergi	*allergy*	Arab	*Arab*
alkohol	*alcohol*	arti	*meaning*
alpukat	*avocado*	asal	*origin*
alun-alun	*square* (loc.)	asam	*sour*
ambil	*take* (v.)	asin	*salty*
ambilkan	*to fetch*	asing	*foreign*
ambulans	*ambulance*	atas	*above,* (coll.) *upstairs*
Amerika	*America*	atau	*or*
Amerika Serikat	*USA*	Australia	*Australia*
anak	*child*	awas	*beware (of)*
anak angkat	*adopted child*	ayah	*father*

ayam	*chicken*	belas	*-teen*
Ayo!	*Come!, Come on!*	beli	*buy*
babi	*pig*	beliau	*he/she, him/her, his/her*
badan	*body*		(formal)
bagaimana	*how*	belok	*to turn*
bagaimana kalau	*how would it be if, (coll.)*	belum	*not yet*
	what about	beralergi	*to have an allergy*
bagasi	*luggage*	beralkohol	*containing alcohol*
bagus	*good, well done*	berangkat	*depart*
bahasa	*language*	berapa	*how many*
bahu	*shoulder*	berasal	*come, originate*
baik	*good, well*	berbintang	*starred, star-rated*
Baiklah.	*All right., Okay.*	berhenti	*stop* (v.)
baju	*clothing*	berikut	*following, next*
baju dalam	*underclothes*	berjalan-jalan	*walking about*
bak mandi	*bathtub*	berkata	*say* (v.)
bakar	*to roast/grill*	berkenalan	*to become acquainted*
bandar udara	*airport*	berlatih	*train* (v.)
bandara	*airport*	berlibur	*to be on vacation*
bank	*bank*	bermain	*play* (v.)
bantu	*help* (v.), *assist* (v.)	bermata	*to have … eyes*
bantuan	*help* (n.)	bersama	*together, (along) with*
Bapak	*Sir, Mr*	berselam skuba	*scuba diving* (v.)
bapak	*Father*	berselancar	*surfing*
barang	*thing, object, goods*	bertemu	*meet* (v.)
barat	*West*	bertetangga	*be/become neighbours*
baru	*new, recently, just, newly*	berumur	*to be aged*
batas	*limit*	besar	*large*
baterai	*dry-cell battery*	besok	*tomorrow*
bawa	*to carry, to take (away)*	betul	*correct*
bawah	*below, (coll.) downstairs*	biasanya	*usually*
bawah tanah	*underground*	bibi	*aunt*
bayam	*spinach*	bibir	*lip, lips*
bayar	*pay* (v.)	bicara	*speak, converse*
bayi	*baby*	bidan	*midwife*
bebas	*be free*	bilang	*say* (coll., v.)
bebek	*duck* (n.)	bioskop	*cinema*
begini	*like this*	bir	*beer*
begitu	*like that*	biru	*blue*
belajar	*study* (v.)	bis	*bus*
belakang	*back* (loc.)	bisa	*can, able to*
belanja	*shop* (v.)	boleh	*may, to be allowed to*
belanjaan	*shopping* (n.)	bolu	*sponge (cake)*

bon	*cheque, bill*	Desember	*December*
botol	*bottle*	di	*at/in/on*
brankas	*safe* (n.)	dia	*he/she, him/her,*
buah	*fruit,* (thing classifier)		*his/her*
buat	*do (something)*	dibawa pulang	*to be taken home*
buatkan	*create (for)*	dibungkus	*to be wrapped*
bubur	*porridge*	diinfus	*to be put on an IV drip*
bukan	*no, not*	dijual	*for sale, to be sold*
buku	*book*	dilarang	*forbidden*
bulan	*month*	dingin	*cold*
bulu tangkis	*badminton*	dioperasi	*to be operated on*
bundaran	*roundabout*	dirawat	*be nursed, treated, cared*
bungkus	*to wrap*		*for*
burung	*bird*	dirawat jalan	*be cared for as an*
cangkir	*cup*		*outpatient*
cara	*method*	dirawat inap	*be cared for as an*
cari	*look for, search for*		*inpatient*
catur	*chess*	dironsen	*to be x-rayed*
celana	*trousers*	diskon	*discount*
cepat	*quick*	dokter	*doctor*
cepat-cepat	*quickly*	dokter anak	*paediatrician*
cerita	*story*	dokter gigi	*dentist*
Cina	*China*	dokter umum	*general practitioner*
coba	*to try* (v.)	domba	*sheep*
coklat	*brown*	dua	*two*
cucu	*grandchild*	duduk	*sit*
dada	*chest*	ekor	*tail,* (animal classifier)
daging	*meat*	ekstra	*extra*
dah	*goodbye*	elektronik	*electronic*
dalam	*inside, within, in*	emas	*gold*
dan	*and*	empat	*four*
danau	*lake*	enak	*delicious*
dapur	*kitchen*	enam	*six*
dari	*from*	Eropa	*Europe*
daripada	*than*	es	*ice, iced*
dasi	*tie*	eskalator	*escalator*
datang	*come, arrive*	fasilitas	*amenity, facility*
dekat	*near*	Februari	*February*
delapan	*eight*	feri	*ferry*
dengan	*with*	film	*film*
dengar	*to hear*	flu	*flu, influenza*
depan	*front, ahead*	fotokopi	*photocopy*
desa	*village*	gamelan	*drum and percussion*

	ensemble	ilmuwan	*scientist*
gang	*alley*	India	*India*
ganti	*switch* (v.), *change* (v.)	infus	*intravenous (IV) therapy*
garam	*salt*	Inggris	*England*
gatal	*itch* (v., n.)	ingin	*want, wish* (v.)
gawai	*work* (n.)	ini	*this*
gayung	*(water) dipper*	insinyur	*engineer*
gelas	*glass*	Irlandia	*Ireland*
gemuk	*plump*	istri	*wife*
gereja	*church*	itu	*that*
gigi	*tooth*	jadi	*so, thus, therefore*
goreng	*to fry*	jagung	*corn*
gratis	*free*	jalan	*street, road, way, walk*
gunung	*mountain*		(v.)
habis	*depleted, all gone*	jalan kaki	*walk, travel on foot*
halaman	*yard, garden, page*	jam	*hour, clock*
halo	*hello, (telephone*	jangan	*do not* (imperative)
	greeting)	janji	*(coll.) appointment*
halte bis	*bus stop*	jantung	*heart*
hamil	*to be pregnant*	Januari	*January*
hangat	*warm*	jarang	*rarely*
hanya	*only*	jari	*finger*
harga	*price, value*	jari kaki	*toe*
hari	*day*	jas	*blazer, coat*
harus	*must*	jatuh	*fall (down)*
hati	*liver,* (fig.) *heart*	jauh	*far*
hati-hati	*carefully, to be careful*	Jawa	*Java*
haus	*thirsty*	jembatan	*bridge*
hidung	*nose*	Jepang	*Japan*
hijau	*green*	jeruk	*orange*
hitam	*black*	jual	*sell*
hotel	*hotel*	juga	*too, also*
HP	*hand phone*	Juli	*July*
hubungi	*contact* (v.)	Jum'at	*Friday*
ibu	*mother*	Juni	*June*
Ibu	*Madam, Mrs, Ms*	jurusan	*destination, heading*
ibu jari	*thumb*		(for)
ibu jari kaki	*big toe*	jus	*juice*
ibu rumah	*housewife*	juta	*million*
tangga		kabar	*news*
ikan	*fish*	kacang	*nut, pea, bean*
iklan	*advertisement*	kacang tanah	*peanut*
ikut	*follow*	kadang-kadang	*sometimes*

kain	*cloth*	kedua	*second*
kakak	*older sibling*	kedutaan	*embassy*
kakek	*grandfather*	keju	*cheese*
kaki	*leg*	kelapa	*coconut*
kalau	*if, when*	keluar	*exit* (v.)
kali	*(number of) times/ occasions*	keluarga	*family*
		kemarin	*yesterday*
kalian	*you, your* (plural, informal)	kembali	*return* (v.)
		Kembali.	*(Thanks) in return., You're welcome.*
kamar dobel	*double room*		
kamar kecil	*toilet* (fig.)	kemeja	*shirt*
kamar kos	*bedsit*	kemudian	*then*
kamar mandi	*bathroom*	kenal	*recognise, know*
kamar singel	*single room*	kenalan	*acquaintance*
kambing	*goat*	Kenalkan.	*Let me introduce you.*
kami	*we/us/our* (exclusive)	kenalkan	*to acquaint (someone)*
Kamis	*Thursday*	kenapa	*why*
kampung	*village*	kendaraan	*vehicle*
kamu	*you, your*	kendaraan umum	*public transport*
Kanada	*Canada*	kentang	*potato*
kanan	*right*	kenyang	*full* (as in *sated*)
kanguru	*kangaroo*	kepada	*to (someone)*
kantor	*office*	kepala	*head*
kantor polisi	*police station*	kepiting	*crab*
kantor pos	*post office*	keponakan	*niece, nephew*
kaos	*t-shirt*	kepulauan	*archipelago*
kaos kaki	*socks*	kereta api	*train*
kapal	*ship*	kerja	*to work*
kapal terbang	*aeroplane*	kesehatan	*health*
Kapan	*When* (interrogative)	ketiga	*third*
karcis	*ticket*	ketika	*when*
kare	*curry*	khas	*typical, specialty (of)*
karena	*because*	khawatir	*worry*
kartu	*card*	khitanan	*circumcision ceremony*
karyawan	*worker, employee*	khusus	*special, exclusive, particular*
Kasihan!	*What a pity!, Poor thing!*		
kasir	*cashier, till* (coll.)	kira-kira	*roughly, at a guess*
ke	*to*	kiri	*left*
kecap	*soy sauce*	kita	*we/us/our* (inclusive)
kecelakaan	*accident*, (coll.) *have an accident*	kode pos	*postcode*
		kolam	*pool, pond*
kecil	*small*	kolega	*colleague*
kedelai	*soy*	koneksi	*connection*

konfirmasi	*confirmation*	lupa	*forget*
koper	*suitcase*	lurus	*straight*
kopi	*coffee*	lusa	*day after tomorrow*
kosong	*zero, empty*	lutut	*knee*
kota	*town, city*	luwak	*civet*
kredit	*credit*	Maaf.	*Sorry.*
krupuk	*cracker*	mahal	*expensive*
kue	*cake*	makan	*eat*
kuku	*nail* (body part)	makan malam	*dinner, eat dinner*
kukus	*to steam*	makan pagi	*breakfast, eat breakfast*
kuli	*unskilled labourer,*	makan siang	*lunch, eat lunch*
	porter	makanan	*food*
kulit	*skin*	makan-makan	*eating (for pleasure)*
kuning	*yellow*	mal	*mall*
kurang	*not quite, less, minus*	malam	*evening, night*
kursi roda	*wheelchair*	mana	*where*
lada	*pepper*	manajer	*manager*
lagi	*again, more*	mandi	*bathe, shower* (v.)
lahir	*to be born*	mangga	*mango*
laki-laki	*man, male*	mangkok	*bowl*
lalu	*past, then*	manis	*sweet*
lama	*old, of long duration*	mantri	*paramedic*
lampu	*light, lamp*	Maret	*March*
lampu merah	*red light,* (coll.) *traffic*	Mari	*Let's, Come*
	light	masak	*cook* (v.)
lantai	*floor, level*	masakan	*cuisine, cooking* (n.)
lapar	*hungry*	masih	*still*
laut	*sea*	masjid	*mosque*
lebih	*more*	masuk	*enter*
leher	*neck*	mata kaki	*ankle*
lengan	*arm*	mau	*want*
letoi	*tired*	Mei	*May*
lewat	*past*	meja	*desk, table*
licin	*slippery*	meja	*table*
lift	*lift*	melati	*jasmine*
lihat	*see, look at*	Melayu	*Malay*
lima	*five*	melukis	*paint* (v.)
loket	*(ticket) window, counter*	membaca	*reading*
lontong	*steamed rice cake*	memberikan	*give (something)*
losmen	*guesthouse*	memesan	*book* (v.), *order* (v.)
LSM	*NGO*	menari	*dance* (v.)
luar	*outside*	mendaki	*climb* (v.)
luka	*wound, cut, injury*	mendengarkan	*listen to*

menderita	suffer	nomor	number
meneliti	research (v.)	Nopember	November
menelpon	call (v.), ring (v.)	November	November
mengajar	teach	numpang tanya…	may I ask…
mengeja	spell (v.)	nyala	ablaze
mengerti	understand	nyamuk	mosquito
menginap	stay (overnight)	obat	medicine, drug
menikah	be/get married	ojek	motorcycle service
menit	minute	Oktober	October
menonton	watch (v.)	oleh	by
menyeberang	cross (v.)	oleh-oleh	souvenir
menyenangkan	pleases, pleasing (v., adj.)	om	uncle
		operasi	operation
merah	red	orang	person, (people classifier)
mereka	they, them, their		
merepotkan	imposing on, overburdening	orang tua	parents
		oranye	orange
mineral	mineral	pada	at, on, in
minggu	week	pagi	morning
Minggu	Sunday	pahit	bitter
minta	request, ask for	pakai	wear, use
minum	drink (v.)	pakaian	clothing
minuman	drink (n.)	paling	most
minum-minum	drinking (alcoholic beverages)	paman	uncle
		pamit	take one's leave
mobil	car	panas	hot
muda	young	pancuran mandi	bathroom shower
muka	face	panggang	to roast/grill
mulai	to start	panggil	to call (by name)
mulut	mouth	panjang	long
muntah	to vomit	pantai	beach
murah	cheap	papan	board
musik	music	parkir	to park
naik	get on, ascend, (coll.) ride/take	pas	to fit, accurate, exactly
		pasar	market
nama	name	pasien	patient
nanti	later	paspor	passport
negara	state, country	pasta gigi	toothpaste
nenek	grandmother	patah tulang	bone fracture
nganga	gaping, wide open	pedas	spicy
ngantuk	sleepy	pegawai	worker, employee
ngeri	scary	pegawai negeri	civil servant
nol	zero	pekerja	worker

pekerjaan	job, occupation	pesawat terbang	aeroplane
pekerjaan rumah	homework	peta	map
pelajar	student	pinggang	waist
pelan	slow	pinggul	hip
pelan-pelan	slowly	pipi	cheek
pelukis	painter	piring	plate
pembantu	servant, helper	pisang	banana
pembuat	maker	pisau	knife
pemesanan	reservation	ponsel	cell phone
pena	pen	potong	slice (v., n.), cut (v., n.)
penari	dancer	praktik	(medical) practice, to practice (medicine)
pencak silat	Indonesian martial arts		
pendek	short	pukul	strike (v.), hour (fig.)
peneliti	researcher	pulang	return home
pengajar	educator	pulau	island
pengering	dryer	puluh	tens digit
penginapan	commercially-run accommodation	punggung	back (body part)
		punya	have, possess, own
penjual	vendor, seller	pusat	shopping centre
penumpang	passenger	perbelanjaan	
penyeberangan	crossing (n.)	pusing	light-headed
per malam	per night	puskesmas	public clinic
perahu	boat	putih	white
perak	silver	Rabu	Wednesday
perawat	nurse	radio	radio
perempatan	intersection, crossroad	ramah	friendly, warm
perempuan	woman, female	rambut	hair
pergelangan tangan	wrist	ranjang	cot, bed
		rasa (n.)	flavour, taste, feel
pergi	go (v.)	rasa (v.)	sense, feel
periksa	to examine	ratus	hundred
perjalanan	trip, journey	rawat	nurse (v.), care for (v.)
perlu	need	rawat inap	inpatient care
permisi	excuse me/us	rawat jalan	outpatient care
pernah	ever	rebus	to boil
persimpangan	intersection	renang	swim (v.)
pertama	first, firstly	repot	busy, overburdened
pertigaan	T-junction	resep	prescription, recipe
perusahaan	company, corporation	resepsionis	receptionist
perut	stomach	reservasi	reservation
pesan (n.)	message	restoran	restaurant
pesan (v.)	order	ribu	thousand
pesanan	order (n.)	rok	skirt

rokok	cigarette	sejak	since
ronsen	x-ray	sekali	once, one time
roti	bread	sekali (adv.)	very
ruko	shophouse	sekarang	now
rumah	house, home	sekolah	school
rumah kos	boarding house	selalu	always
rumah makan	eatery, restaurant	selama	for a duration of
rumah sakit	hospital	Selamat datang!	Welcome!
rumah tangga	household	Selamat jalan	Have a good journey!
rusa	deer	Selamat malam!	Good evening/night!
Sabtu	Saturday	Selamat pagi!	Good morning!
sagu	sago	Selamat siang!	Good day!
saja	merely, only	Selamat sore!	Good afternoon!
sakit	be ill, be sick, ache, hurt, pain	Selamat tinggal	Goodbye! (when leaving)
salah	incorrect, wrong	Selandia Baru	New Zealand
Salam	Regards	Selasa	Tuesday
Sama-sama.	Likewise., You're welcome.	selesai	to be finished, to be done
sambal	chilli paste	seluler	cellular
sampai	arrive, until	semalam	a night
sampaikan	pass (something) on	sembarangan	carelessly
samping	side	sembilan	nine
sana	over there	sembuh	recover, get well again
santan	coconut milk	semoga	hope that
saos	sauce	semua	all
sapi	cow	senang	enjoy, to be pleased
sate	meat skewer	sendal	sandal
satu	one	sendiri	oneself
saudara	relative, sibling	sendok garpu	cutlery
saya	I, me, my	seni	craft, art
sayur	vegetable	Senin	Monday
sebaiknya	it is best that…	seorang	one person (classifier)
sebelah	side	sepak bola	football
sebelas	eleven	sepasang	a pair of
sebelum	before	sepatu	shoe
sebentar	a moment	sepeda	bicycle
seberang	other side	sepeda motor	motorcycle
sebuah	one thing (classifier)	seperempat	a quarter
sedang	currently	September	September
sedotan	straw	sepuluh	ten
sehari-hari	everyday (adj.)	sepupu	cousin
sehat	healthy	sering	often

sesudah	after	tangga	staircase
setengah	half	tanggal	(calendar) date
setiap	every	tanpa	without, lacking
setrika	iron (appliance)	tante	aunt
sewa	rent (v.)	tanya	ask, enquire
sewaktu	while	tarif	rate, fee, fare
siang	daytime (11a.m.–3p.m.)	tas	bag
siapa	who	tawar	plain, unsweetened
sibuk	busy	tebus	to redeem
sikat	brush	teh	tea
siku	elbow	telefon	telephone
silakan	please, go ahead	telepon	telephone
singa	lion	televisi	television
Singapura	Singapore	telinga	ear
singkong	cassava	telpon	telephone
sini	here	telur	egg
situ	there	teman	friend
Skotlandia	Scotland	tempat	place, location
sombong	snobbish	tempat tidur	bed
sop	soup	tempe	fermented soy bean cake
sore	afternoon		
stasiun	station	tengah	centre, middle
suami	husband	tenggorokan	throat
sudah	already	tentu	of course
suka	like (v.)	terakhir	last, finally
sumpit	chopsticks	teras	porch
Suster	Sister	terbuka	opened
susu	milk	Terima kasih.	Thank you.
swalayan	self-service	terlalu	too, overly
swasta	private (non - governmental)	terlambat	slow, late
		termasuk	included
syair	quatrain, poetry	tersebut	mentioned, said
syal	shawl	tersesat	to be lost
syukuran	thanksgiving	terus	(continue) onwards
tadi	earlier	tetangga	neighbour
tahu (v.)	know, be aware (of)	tetapi	but
tahu (n.)	tofu	tidak	no, not
tahun	year	Tidak ada apa-apa.	Nothing's the matter.
taksi	taxi		
takut	afraid of, nervous about	Tidak apa-apa.	It's nothing., No worries.
tamu	guest	tidak enak badan	unwell
tanah	ground	tidak pernah	never
tangan	hand	tidak usah	no need to

tidur	*sleep* (v.)	udang	*prawn, shrimp*
tiga	*three*	ukuran	*size*
tiket	*ticket*	ulang	*repeat*
timur	*east*	ulang tahun	*birthday*
tinggal	*live, reside, remain*	umur	*age*
tinggi	*tall*	Unit Gawat Darurat	*Emergency Unit*
titip	*entrust*		
toko	*shop, store*	ungu	*purple*
topi	*hat*	universitas	*university*
toserba	*department store*	untuk	*for, for the purpose of*
tradisional	*traditional*	vespa	*scooter*
trotoar	*pavement*	Wah	expression of awe
tua	*old*	wajan	*wok*
tugu	*monument*	waktu	*time* (n.)
tujuh	*seven*	Wales	*Wales*
tukang	*skilled labourer, handyman*	warna	*colour*
		warnet	*internet café*
tumis	*to stir-fry*	wartawan	*journalist*
tunggu	*wait*	warung	*street stall*
turun	*get off, descend*	ya	*yes*
uang	*money (also notes and coins)*	yang	*that, which, that which*
uang kembalian	*change*	Yang mana?	*Which one/ones?*
uang tunai	*cash*	YTH	*Dear* (form of address)

English–Indonesian glossary

If an Indonesian word has been presented in more than one form in the book, you'll find both forms listed under the same entry. For example, when you look up the word *work*, you'll find both **kerja** and **bekerja**.

(interrogative in yes/no questions)	*Apakah*	all	*semua*
		All right.	*Baiklah.*
(telephone greeting)	*halo*	allergy	*alergi*
ablaze	*nyala*	alley	*gang*
able to	*bisa*	allowed	*boleh*
above	*atas*	already	*sudah*
accident	*kecelakaan*	also	*juga*
accommodation	*akomodasi*	always	*selalu*
(commercially-run) accommodation	*penginapan*	ambulance	*ambulans*
		amenity	*fasilitas*
accountant	*akuntan*	America	*Amerika*
accurate	*pas*	and	*dan*
ache	*sakit*	ankle	*mata kaki*
acquaint (someone)	*kenalkan*	antibiotic	*antibiotik*
acquaintance	*kenalan*	antiseptic	*antiseptik*
activity	*kegiatan*	appointment	(coll.) *janji*
address	*alamat*	April	*April*
adopted child	*anak angkat*	Arab	*Arab*
advertisement	*iklan*	archipelago	*kepulauan*
aeroplane	*kapal terbang, pesawat terbang*	arm	*lengan*
		arrive	*sampai*
afraid (of)	*takut*	arrive	*datang*
after	*sesudah*	art	*seni*
afternoon	*sore*	ascend	*naik*
again	*lagi*	ask	*tanya*
age	*umur*	assist (v.)	*bantu, membantu*
aged	*berumur*	at (loc.)	*di*
ahead	*depan*	at (time period)	*pada*
airport	*bandar udara, bandara*	at a guess	*kira-kira*
		August	*Agustus*
alcohol	*alkohol*	aunt	*bibi, tante*

Australia	*Australia*	bill	*bon*
available	*ada*	bird	*burung*
avocado	*alpukat*	birthday	*ulang tahun*
aware (of)	*tahu*	bitter	*pahit*
baby	*bayi*	black	*hitam*
back (body part)	*punggung*	blazer	*jas*
back (loc.)	*belakang*	blue	*biru*
badminton	*bulu tangkis*	board	*papan*
bag	*tas*	boarding house	*rumah kos*
bamboo musical	*angklung*	boat	*perahu*
instrument		body	*badan*
banana	*pisang*	boil (v.)	*rebus*
bank	*bank*	bone fracture	*patah tulang*
bathe	*mandi*	book	*buku*
bathroom	*kamar mandi*	book (v.)	*memesan*
bathtub	*bak mandi*	born	*lahir*
be cared for	*dirawat*	bottle	*botol*
be nursed	*dirawat*	bowl	*mangkok*
be on vacation	*berlibur*	bread	*roti*
be operated on	*dioperasi*	breakfast	*makan pagi*
be put on an IV drip	*diinfus*	bridge	*jembatan*
be treated as an	*dirawat inap*	brown	*coklat*
inpatient		brush	*sikat*
be treated as an	*dirawat jalan*	bus	*bis*
outpatient		bus stop	*halte bis*
be x-rayed	*dironsen*	busy	*sibuk, repot*
be/become	*bertetangga*	but	*tetapi*
neighbours		buy	*beli*
beach	*pantai*	by	*oleh*
bean	*kacang*	cake	*kue*
because	*karena*	call (by name)	*panggil*
become acquainted	*berkenalan*	call (v.)	*menelpon*
bed	*tempat tidur,*	can (v.)	*bisa*
	ranjang	Canada	*Kanada*
bedsit	*kamar kos*	car	*mobil*
beef	*daging sapi*	card	*kartu*
beer	*bir*	care for (v.)	*rawat, merawat*
before	*sebelum*	careful	*hati-hati*
below	*bawah*	carefully	*hati-hati*
between	*antara*	carelessly	*sembarangan*
beware (of)	*awas*	carry	*bawa*
bicycle	*sepeda*	cash	*uang tunai*
big toe	*ibu jari kaki*	cashier	*kasir*

cassava	*singkong*	connection	*koneksi*
cell phone	*ponsel*	contact (v.)	*hubungi*
cellular	*seluler*	continuing	*terus*
centre	*tengah*	converse	*bicara*
change	*uang kembalian*	cook (v.)	*masak, memasak*
change (v.)	*ganti*	cooking (n.)	*masakan*
cheap	*murah*	corn	*jagung*
cheek	*pipi*	corporation	*perusahaan*
cheese	*keju*	correct	*betul*
cheque	*bon*	cot	*ranjang*
chess	*catur*	counter	*loket*
chest	*dada*	country	*negara*
chicken	*ayam*	cousin	*sepupu*
child	*anak*	cow	*sapi*
chilli paste	*sambal*	crab	*kepiting*
China	*Cina*	cracker	*krupuk*
chopsticks	*sumpit*	craft	*seni*
church	*gereja*	create (for)	*buatkan*
cigarette	*rokok*	credit	*kredit*
cinema	*bioskop*	cross (v.)	*menyeberang*
circumcision	*khitanan*	crossing (n.)	*penyeberangan*
ceremony		crossroad	*perempatan*
city	*kota*	cuisine	*masakan*
civet	*luwak*	cup	*cangkir*
civil servant	*pegawai negeri*	currently	*sedang*
clear (v.)	*(coll.) angkat*	curry	*kare*
climb (v.)	*mendaki*	cut (n.)	*luka*
clock	*jam*	cut (v., n.)	*potong*
cloth	*kain*	cutlery	*sendok garpu*
clothing	*baju, pakaian*	dance (v.)	*menari*
coconut	*kelapa*	dancer	*penari*
coconut milk	*santan*	date (calendar)	*tanggal*
coffee	*kopi*	day	*hari*
cold	*dingin*	day after tomorrow	*lusa*
colleague	*kolega*	daytime (11a.m.–3p.m.)	*siang*
colour	*warna*	Dear (form of address)	*YTH*
come	*datang*	December	*Desember*
come (from)	*berasal*	deer	*rusa*
Come …	*Mari*	delicious	*enak*
Come on!	*Ayo!*	dentist	*dokter gigi*
Come!	*Ayo!*	depart	*berangkat*
company	*perusahaan*	department store	*toserba*
confirmation	*konfirmasi*	depleted	*habis*

descend	*turun*	end (n.)	*akhir*
desk	*meja*	engineer	*insinyur*
destination	*jurusan*	England	*Inggris*
dinner	*makan malam*	enjoy	*senang*
(water) dipper	*gayung*	enquire	*tanya*
discount	*diskon*	enter	*masuk*
do (something)	*buat, berbuat*	entrust	*titip*
do not (imperative)	*jangan*	escalator	*eskalator*
doctor	*dokter*	escort	*antar*
done	*selesai*	Europe	*Eropa*
double room	*kamar dobel*	evening	*malam*
downstairs	*(coll.) bawah*	ever	*pernah*
drink	*minuman*	every	*setiap*
drink (v.)	*minum*	everyday (adj.)	*sehari-hari*
drinking (alcoholic beverages)	*minum-minum*	exactly	*pas*
		examine	*periksa*
drug	*obat*	exclusive	*khusus*
drum and percussion ensemble	*gamelan*	excuse me/us	*permisi*
		exit (v.)	*keluar*
dry-cell battery	*baterai*	expensive	*mahal*
dryer	*pengering*	expression of awe	*Wah*
duck (n.)	*bebek*	extra	*ekstra*
ear	*telinga*	face	*muka*
earlier	*tadi*	facility	*fasilitas*
east	*timur*	fall (down)	*jatuh*
eat	*makan*	family	*keluarga*
eat breakfast	*makan pagi*	far	*jauh*
eat dinner	*makan malam*	fare	*tarif*
eat lunch	*makan siang*	father	*ayah*
eatery	*rumah makan*	father	*bapak*
eating (for pleasure)	*makan-makan*	February	*Februari*
educator	*pengajar*	fee	*tarif*
egg	*telur*	feel (n.)	*rasa*
eight	*delapan*	feel (v.)	*rasa, merasa*
elbow	*siku*	female	*perempuan*
electronic	*elektronik*	fermented soy bean cake	*tempe*
eleven	*sebelas*		
embassy	*kedutaan*	ferry	*feri*
Emergency Unit	*Unit Gawat Darurat*	fetch	*ambilkan*
		few	*sedikit*
employee	*pekerja, karyawan, pegawai*	film	*film*
		finally	*terakhir*
empty	*kosong*	finger	*jari*

finished	*selesai*	gold	*emas*
fire	*api*	good	*bagus, baik*
first	*pertama*	Good afternoon!	*Selamat sore!*
firstly	*pertama*	Good day!	*Selamat siang!*
fish	*ikan*	Good evening/night!	*Selamat malam!*
fit (v.)	*pas*	Good morning!	*Selamat pagi!*
five	*lima*	goodbye	*dah*
flavour (n.)	*rasa*	Goodbye! (when	*Selamat tinggal!*
floor	*lantai*	leaving)	
flu	*flu*	goods	*barang*
follow	*ikut*	grandchild	*cucu*
following (adj.)	*berikut*	grandfather	*kakek*
food	*makanan*	grandmother	*nenek*
football	*sepak bola*	green	*hijau*
for	*untuk*	grey	*abu-abu*
for (a duration of)	*selama*	ground	*tanah*
for sale	*dijual*	guest	*tamu*
for (the purpose of)	*untuk*	guesthouse	*losmen*
forbidden	*dilarang*	hair	*rambut*
foreign	*asing*	half	*setengah*
forget	*lupa*	hand	*tangan*
four	*empat*	hand phone	*HP*
be free	*bebas*	handyman	*tukang*
free	*gratis*	has/have	*ada*
Friday	*Jum'at*	hat	*topi*
friend	*teman*	have	*punya*
friendly	*ramah*	have … eyes	*bermata*
from	*dari*	Have a good journey!	*Selamat jalan!*
front	*depan*	have an accident	*(coll.) kecelakaan*
fruit	*buah*	have an allergy	*beralergi*
fry (v.)	*goreng*	he	*dia, beliau (formal)*
full (as in sated)	*kenyang*	head	*kepala*
garden	*halaman*	heading (for)	*jurusan*
general practitioner	*dokter umum*	health	*kesehatan*
get off	*turun*	healthy	*sehat*
get on	*naik*	hear (v.)	*dengar*
get well again	*sembuh*	heart	*jantung, (fig.) hati*
give (something)	*memberikan*	hello	*halo*
glass	*gelas*	help (n.)	*bantuan*
go (v.)	*pergi*	help (v.)	*bantu, membantu*
go ahead	*silakan*	helper	*pembantu*
goat	*kambing*	her	*dia, beliau (formal)*
going to	*akan*	here	*sini*

him	*dia, beliau (formal)*	Ireland	*Irlandia*
hip	*pinggul*	iron (appliance)	*setrika*
his	*dia, beliau (formal)*	island	*pulau*
home	*rumah*	it is best that …	*sebaiknya*
homework	*pekerjaan rumah*	It's nothing.	*Tidak apa-apa.*
hope that	*semoga*	itch (v., n.)	*gatal*
hospital	*rumah sakit*	January	*Januari*
hot	*panas*	Japan	*Jepang*
hotel	*hotel*	jasmine	*melati*
hour	*jam*	Java	*Jawa*
hour (fig.)	*pukul*	job	*pekerjaan*
house	*rumah*	journalist	*wartawan*
household	*rumah tangga*	journey	*perjalanan*
housewife	*ibu rumah tangga*	juice	*jus*
how	*bagaimana*	July	*Juli*
How are you?	*Apa kabar?*	June	*Juni*
how many	*berapa*	just	*baru*
how would it be if	*bagaimana kalau*	kangaroo	*kanguru*
hundred	*ratus*	kitchen	*dapur*
hungry	*lapar*	knee	*lutut*
hurt	*sakit*	knife	*pisau*
husband	*suami*	know	*tahu*
I	*aku (informal),*	know (someone)	*kenal*
	saya (formal)	labourer (skilled)	*tukang*
ice	*es*	labourer (unskilled)	*kuli*
if	*kalau*	lacking	*tanpa*
ill	*sakit*	lamb	*daging anak*
imposing on	*merepotkan*		*domba*
in (fig.)	*dalam*	lake	*danau*
in (loc.)	*di*	lamp	*lampu*
in (time period)	*pada*	language	*bahasa*
included	*termasuk*	large	*besar*
incorrect	*salah*	last	*terakhir*
India	*India*	late (v.)	*terlambat*
influenza	*flu*	later	*nanti*
injury	*luka*	left	*kiri*
inpatient care	*rawat inap*	leg	*kaki*
inside	*dalam*	less	*kurang*
internet café	*warnet*	Let me introduce you.	*Kenalkan.*
intersection	*persimpangan,*	Let's	*Mari*
	perempatan	level	*lantai*
intravenous (IV)	*infus*	lift	*lift*
therapy		lift (up)	*angkat*

light-headed	*pusing*	meat skewer	*sate*
like (v.)	*suka*	medicine	*obat*
like that	*begitu*	meet (v.)	*bertemu*
like this	*begini*	mentioned (adj.)	*tersebut*
Likewise.	*Sama-sama.*	merely	*saja*
limit	*batas*	message (n.)	*pesan*
lion	*singa*	method	*cara*
lip(s)	*bibir*	middle	*tengah*
listen to	*mendengarkan*	midwife	*bidan*
a little	*sedikit*	milk	*susu*
live (v.)	*tinggal*	million	*juta*
liver	*hati*	mineral	*mineral*
location	*tempat*	minus	*kurang*
long	*panjang*	minute	*menit*
long duration (of)	*lama*	(a) moment	*sebentar*
look at	*lihat*	Monday	*Senin*
look for	*cari, mencari*	money (*also* notes	*uang*
lost (v.)	*tersesat*	and coins)	
luggage	*bagasi*	month	*bulan*
lunch (n., v.)	*makan siang*	monument	*tugu*
Madam	*Ibu*	more	*lagi*
make	*buat*	more	*lebih*
maker	*pembuat*	morning	*pagi*
Malay	*Melayu*	mosque	*masjid*
male	*laki-laki*	mosquito	*nyamuk*
mall	*mal*	most	*paling*
man	*laki-laki*	mother	*ibu*
manager	*manajer*	motorcycle	*sepeda motor*
mango	*mangga*	motorcycle service	*ojek*
many	*banyak*	mountain	*gunung*
map	*peta*	mouth	*mulut*
March	*Maret*	Mrs	*Ibu*
market	*pasar*	Ms	*Ibu*
married (be/get)	*menikah*	much	*banyak*
martial arts	*pencak silat*	music	*musik*
(Indonesian)		must	*harus*
May	*Mei*	mutton	*daging domba*
may	*boleh*	my	*aku (informal),*
may I ask ...	*numpang tanya ...*		*saya (formal)*
me	*aku (informal),*	nail (body part)	*kuku*
	saya (formal)	name	*nama*
meaning	*arti*	near	*dekat*
meat	*daging*	neck	*leher*

need	*perlu*	on (loc.)	*di*
neighbour	*tetangga*	on (time period)	*pada*
nephew	*keponakan laki-laki*	once	*sekali*
		one	*satu*
nervous (about)	*takut*	one time/occasion	*sekali*
never	*tidak pernah*	oneself	*sendiri*
new	*baru*	only	*saja*
New Zealand	*Selandia Baru*	only	*hanya*
newly	*baru*	(continue) onwards	*terus*
news	*kabar*	opened	*terbuka*
next	*berikut*	operation	*operasi*
NGO	*LSM*	or	*atau*
niece	*keponakan perempuan*	(the colour) orange	*oranye*
		orange	*jeruk*
night	*malam*	orangeade	*air jeruk*
a night	*semalam*	order (n.)	*pesanan*
nine	*sembilan*	order (v.)	*pesan, memesan*
no	*bukan, tidak*	origin	*asal*
no need to	*tidak usah*	originate	*berasal*
No worries.	*Tidak apa-apa.*	other side	*seberang*
nose	*hidung*	our	*kami, kita*
not	*bukan, tidak*	outpatient care	*rawat jalan*
not quite	*kurang*	outside	*luar*
not yet	*belum*	overburdened	*repot*
Nothing's the matter.	*Tidak ada apa-apa.*	overburdening	*merepotkan*
		overly	*terlalu*
November	*Nopember*	own (v.)	*punya*
November	*November*	paediatrician	*dokter anak*
now	*sekarang*	page	*halaman*
number	*nomor*	pain	*sakit*
nurse	*perawat*	paint (v.)	*melukis*
nurse (v.)	*rawat, merawat*	painter	*pelukis*
nut	*kacang*	(a) pair of	*sepasang*
object	*barang*	paramedic	*mantri*
(number of) occasion	*kali*	parents	*orang tua*
occupation	*pekerjaan*	park (v.)	*parkir*
October	*Oktober*	particular	*khusus*
of course	*tentu*	pass (something) on	*sampaikan*
office	*kantor*	passenger	*penumpang*
often	*sering*	passport	*paspor*
Okay.	*Baiklah.*	past	*lalu, lewat*
old	*tua*	patient	*pasien*
old (of long duration)	*lama*	pavement	*trotoar*

pay (v.)	*bayar*	purple	*ungu*
pea	*kacang*	(a) quarter	*seperempat*
peanut	*kacang tanah*	quatrain	*syair*
pen	*pena*	quick	*cepat*
pepper	*lada*	quickly	*cepat-cepat*
per night	*per malam*	radio	*radio*
person	*orang*	rarely	*jarang*
pharmacy	*apotek*	rate	*tarif*
photocopy	*fotokopi*	reading	*membaca*
pig	*babi*	recently	*baru*
place	*tempat*	receptionist	*resepsionis*
plain	*tawar*	recipe	*resep*
plate	*piring*	recognise	*kenal*
play (v.)	*bermain, main*	recover	*sembuh*
please	*silakan*	red	*merah*
pleased	*senang*	red light	*lampu merah*
pleases	*menyenangkan*	redeem	*tebus*
pleasing (v., adj.)	*menyenangkan*	Regards	*Salam*
plump	*gemuk*	relative	*saudara*
poetry	*syair*	remain	*tinggal*
police station	*kantor polisi*	rent (v.)	*sewa, menyewa*
pond	*kolam*	repeat	*ulang*
pool	*kolam*	request, ask for	*minta*
Poor thing!	*Kasihan!*	research (v.)	*meneliti*
porch	*teras*	researcher	*peneliti*
pork	*daging babi*	reservation	*pemesanan,*
porridge	*bubur*		*reservasi*
porter	*kuli*	reside	*tinggal*
possess	*punya*	restaurant	*restoran, rumah*
post office	*kantor pos*		*makan*
postcode	*kode pos*	return (v.)	*kembali*
potato	*kentang*	return home	*pulang*
(medical) practice	*praktik*	ride	(coll.) *naik*
(v., n.)		right	*kanan*
prawn	*udang*	ring (v.)	*menelpon*
pregnant (v.)	*hamil*	road	*jalan*
prescription	*resep*	roast/grill (v.)	*panggang, bakar*
present (somewhere)	*ada*	roughly	*kira-kira*
price	*harga*	roundabout	*bundaran*
private	*swasta*	safe (n.)	*brankas*
(non - governmental)		sago	*sagu*
public clinic	*puskesmas*	said (adj.)	*tersebut*
public transport	*kendaraan umum*	salt	*garam*

salty	*asin*	sibling	*saudara*
sandal	*sendal*	sibling (older)	*kakak*
Saturday	*'Sabtu*	sibling (younger)	*adik*
sauce	*saos*	sick	*sakit*
say (v.)	*berkata,* (coll.)	side	*samping, sebelah*
	bilang	silver	*perak*
scary	*ngeri*	since	*sejak*
school	*sekolah*	Singapore	*Singapura*
scientist	*ilmuwan*	single room	*kamar singel*
scooter	*vespa*	Sir, Mr	*Bapak*
Scotland	*Skotlandia*	Sister	*Suster*
scuba diving (v.)	*berselam skuba*	sit	*duduk*
sea	*laut*	six	*enam*
search for	*cari, mencari*	size	*ukuran*
second	*kedua*	skin	*kulit*
see	*lihat*	skirt	*rok*
self-service	*swalayan*	sleep (v.)	*tidur*
sell	*jual*	sleepy	*ngantuk*
seller	*penjual*	slice (v., n.)	*potong*
sense (v.)	*rasa, merasa*	slippery	*licin*
September	*September*	slow	*pelan*
servant	*pembantu*	slowly	*pelan-pelan*
seven	*tujuh*	small	*kecil*
shall	*akan*	snobbish	*sombong*
shawl	*syal*	so	*jadi*
she	*dia, beliau* (formal)	socks	*kaos kaki*
sheep	*domba*	sometimes	*kadang-kadang*
ship	*kapal*	Sorry.	*Maaf.*
shirt	*kemeja*	soup	*sop*
shoe	*sepatu*	sour	*asam*
shop (n.)	*toko*	souvenir	*oleh-oleh*
shop (v.)	*belanja,*	soy	*kedelai*
	berbelanja	soy sauce	*kecap*
shophouse	*ruko*	speak	*bicara*
shopping (n.)	*belanjaan*	special	*khusus*
shopping centre	*pusat*	specialty (of)	*khas*
	perbelanjaan	spell (v.)	*mengeja*
short	*pendek*	spicy	*pedas*
shorts	*celana pendek*	spinach	*bayam*
shoulder	*bahu*	sponge (cake)	*bolu*
shower (bathroom)	*pancuran mandi*	spy	*mata-mata*
shower (v.)	*mandi*	square (loc.)	*alun-alun*
shrimp	*udang*	staircase	*tangga*

star-rated	*berbintang*	television	*televisi*
starred	*berbintang*	ten	*sepuluh*
start (v.)	*mulai*	tens digit	*puluh*
state	*negara*	than	*daripada*
station	*stasiun*	Thank you.	*Terima kasih.*
stay (overnight)	*menginap*	thanksgiving	*syukuran*
steam (v.)	*kukus*	that	*itu*
steamed rice cake	*lontong*	that	*yang*
stepchild	*anak tiri*	that which	*yang*
still	*masih*	their	*mereka*
stir-fry (v., n.)	*tumis*	them	*mereka*
stomach	*perut*	then	*lalu*
stop (v.)	*berhenti*	then	*kemudian*
store (n.)	*toko*	there	*situ*
story	*cerita*	there (over)	*sana*
straight	*lurus*	there is/are	*ada*
straw	*sedotan*	therefore	*jadi*
street	*jalan*	they	*mereka*
street stall	*warung*	thing	*barang*
strike (v.)	*pukul*	third	*ketiga*
student	*pelajar*	thirsty	*haus*
study (v.)	*belajar*	this	*ini*
suffer	*menderita*	thousand	*ribu*
suitcase	*koper*	three	*tiga*
Sunday	*Minggu*	throat	*tenggorokan*
surfing	*berselancar*	thumb	*ibu jari*
sweet	*manis*	Thursday	*Kamis*
swim (v.)	*renang, berenang*	thus	*jadi*
switch (v.)	*ganti*	ticket	*karcis*
table	*meja*	ticket	*tiket*
take (away)	*bawa*	tie	*dasi*
take (transportation)	(coll.) *naik*	till	(coll.) *kasir*
take (v.)	*ambil*	time (n.)	*waktu*
take one's leave	*pamit*	(number of) time	*kali*
taken home	*dibawa pulang*	letoi	*tired*
tall	*tinggi*	T-junction	*pertigaan*
taste (n.)	*rasa*	to	*ke*
taxi	*taksi*	to (someone)	*kepada*
tea	*teh*	today	*hari ini*
teach	*mengajar*	toe	*jari kaki*
-teen	*belas*	tofu	*tahu (n.)*
telephone	*telepon, telpon, telefon*	together	*bersama*

toilet	WC, toilet, (fig.) kamar kecil	waist	pinggang
		wait	tunggu
tomorrow	besok	Wales	Wales
too (also)	juga	walk (v.)	jalan, jalan kaki
too (overly)	terlalu	walking about	berjalan-jalan
tooth	gigi	want	mau
toothpaste	pasta gigi	want	ingin
town	kota	warm	ramah
traditional	tradisional	warm	hangat
traffic light	(coll.) lampu merah	watch (v.)	menonton
		water	air
train	kereta api	way	jalan
train (v.)	berlatih	we	kami, kita
travel on foot	jalan kaki	wear (v.)	pakai
trip (n.)	perjalanan	Wednesday	Rabu
trousers	celana	week	minggu
try (v.)	coba	Welcome!	Selamat datang!
t-shirt	kaos	well	baik
Tuesday	Selasa	well done	bagus
turn (v.)	belok	west	barat
two	dua	what	apa
typical	khas	What a pity!	Kasihan!
uncle	om, paman	what about	(coll.) bagaimana kalau
underclothes	baju dalam		
underground	bawah tanah	What's the matter?	Ada apa?
understand	mengerti	wheelchair	kursi roda
university	universitas	when	ketika, kalau
unsweetened	tawar	When (interrogative)	Kapan
until	sampai	where	mana
unwell	tidak enak badan	whether	apakah
		which	yang
upstairs	(coll.) atas	Which one/ones?	Yang mana?
us	kami, kita	while	sewaktu
USA	Amerika Serikat	white	putih
use (v.)	pakai	who	siapa
usually	biasanya	why	kenapa
value	harga	wife	istri
vegetable	sayur	will	akan
vehicle	kendaraan	window (ticket)	loket
vendor	penjual	wish (v.)	ingin
very	sekali (adv.)	with	dengan
village	desa, kampung	(along) with	bersama
vomit (v.)	muntah	within	dalam

without	*tanpa*	yard	*halaman*
wok	*wajan*	year	*tahun*
woman	*perempuan*	yellow	*kuning*
work (v.)	*kerja, bekerja*	yes	*ya*
worker	*pekerja, karyawan,*	yesterday	*kemarin*
	pegawai	you	*Anda, kamu,*
worry	*khawatir*		*kalian (plural)*
wound	*luka*	You're welcome.	*Sama-sama.*
wrap (v.)	*bungkus*		*Kembali.*
wrapped	*dibungkus*	young	*muda*
wrist	*pergelangan*	your	*Anda, kamu,*
	tangan		*kalian (plural)*
wrong	*salah*	zero	*nol, kosong*
x-ray	*ronsen*		